Meeting Special Nee
in Mainstream Schools

A Practical Guide for Teachers

Second Edition

Richard Stakes and Garry Hornby

David Fulton Publishers Ltd
Ormond House, 26–27 Boswell Street, London WC1N 3JZ

www.fultonpublishers.co.uk

First published in Great Britain by David Fulton Publishers 2000
Reprinted 2001

British Library Cataloguing in Publication Data
A catalogue record for this book is available from the British Library

ISBN 1–85346–699–9

The publishers would like to thank John Cox for copy-editing
and Sophie Cox for proofreading.

Typeset by Mark Heslington, Scarborough, North Yorkshire
Printed in Great Britain by The Cromwell Press Ltd, Trowbridge, Wilts.

Contents

Preface

This book has grown out of the authors' experience of providing training on special educational needs to trainee and experienced teachers in mainstream primary and secondary schools over many years. The purpose of the book is to provide information and practical guidance to such teachers on the teaching of children with special educational needs (SEN).

This is particularly important at this time because of two factors. First, increased awareness of the fact that the majority of children with SEN are already in mainstream schools. Second, the current policy of increasing inclusion within mainstream schools of as many children as possible who are currently in special schools and units. It is therefore now essential that all teachers in mainstream schools become aware of their key role in teaching children with SEN and seek to improve their knowledge and skills in this area.

It is for this reason that the Standards for the Award of Qualified Teacher Status (TTA 1999) include specific reference to SEN and require teachers to be able to:

- identify pupils with SEN;
- know where to get help;
- provide positive and targeted support;
- be familiar with the Code of Practice for SEN;
- implement and keep records on individual education plans (IEPs).

The Code of Practice (DfE 1994a) detailed eight different types of SEN. These are: learning difficulties, specific learning difficulties, emotional and behavioural difficulties, physical disabilities, visual difficulties, hearing difficulties, speech and language difficulties and medical conditions. The QTS standards also include a ninth type of SEN, very able or gifted children.

This book provides information on the identification of all these types of SEN and suggests strategies which will be useful for teachers in mainstream schools when teaching pupils with the different types. It concentrates on practical classroom strategies and activities for mainstream teachers who may have limited knowledge or experience of pupils with SEN.

This book aims to facilitate the development of the key skills, knowledge and understanding required by mainstream teachers. It will also identify key issues in the organisation and management of provision for children with SEN in mainstream schools.

Chapter 1 outlines the development of provision for pupils with SEN in mainstream schools. It outlines the requirements of the Code of Practice, including Statements of special educational need and the elements of Individual Education Plans. The prevalence of SEN is discussed, as is the importance of the mainstream teacher's role in identification of SEN.

Chapter 2 is concerned with the children whose cognitive abilities differ in some way from the norm. It includes children with specific learning difficulties and those with mild, moderate and severe learning difficulties. It also includes children with autism and those considered to be gifted.

Chapter 3 is concerned with teaching children who have hearing or visual difficulties. It provides information on the identification of these SEN and suggests strategies that mainstream class teachers can use in teaching such pupils.

Chapter 4 is concerned with teaching children who have either physical disabilities, medical conditions or communication difficulties. It seeks to provide a basic understanding of these SEN which are increasingly found among children attending mainstream schools.

Chapter 5 focuses on children with emotional and behavioural difficulties. It discusses the characteristics of EBD and provides a review of the different approaches which can be used with children with EBD in mainstream schools.

Chapter 6 is concerned with the assessment of pupils' SEN. It outlines the different purposes of assessment, discusses the use of informal and formal approaches, the major forms of assessment and individual and group tests.

Chapter 7 is concerned with curriculum planning issues. It covers the importance of planning, deciding priorities, the requirements of the National Curriculum and implications for planning from several major theorists including Piaget and Vygotsky.

Chapter 8 considers classroom management issues. It includes a discussion of both appropriate and inappropriate techniques to use with pupils with SEN.

Chapters 9, 10 and 11 consider the key basic skill areas for teachers working with children with SEN. These chapters focus on developing skills in reading, handwriting, spelling and mathematics.

Chapter 12 considers working with parents of children with SEN. It presents a model for parental involvement and suggests various ways in which teachers and parents can work together. It provides suggestions for improving parental involvement in assessments and reviews of progress and outlines the skills needed by teachers in order to work effectively with parents.

Chapter 13 is concerned with whole-school issues, including developing a whole-school policy, working with classroom assistants and other professionals, and other practical issues.

At the end of the book there is a list of addresses of organisations with an interest in SEN and which may be particularly useful to teachers in mainstream schools.

CHAPTER 1

Overview

Introduction

This first chapter provides an overview of relevant information on the teaching of children with special educational needs (SEN) in mainstream schools. It starts with the historical development of mainstream provision for SEN and then explains the current policy regarding the inclusion of children with SEN in mainstream schools. It goes on to provide an outline of the requirements of the National Curriculum, the OFSTED Framework and the Code of Practice for SEN as they affect the mainstream classroom teacher. It presents an explanation of Individual Educational Plans (IEPs) and Statements of SEN. It outlines the various types of SEN and discusses their prevalence in mainstream schools. Finally, it outlines the key role which mainstream teachers play in identifying and meeting SEN.

Historical development

The term special educational needs (SEN) is relatively recent, largely emanating from the language and philosophy of the Warnock Report (DES 1978) which was an important milestone in the development of education for children with SEN in the UK. The concept of SEN is that of an umbrella term, describing a wide range of difficulties which may impair children's ability to achieve during their time in school. Although the phrase is relatively new, awareness of the problems exhibited by such children in school has been widespread from the introduction of compulsory education at the end of the nineteenth century. Since that time teachers have been increasingly aware of the problems presented by such pupils and of their difficulties in addressing them. Reports from HMI and school logbooks over the past 120 years consistently provide evidence of these difficulties (Stakes and Hornby 1997).

Provision for pupils with SEN in mainstream schools has developed gradually over this period. The development of this provision during the last century has been influenced by seven major factors. These are:

- the existence of political will to initiate and sustain developments for pupils with SEN;

- the provision of adequate resources by LEAs to meet the needs of children with SEN in mainstream schools;
- the development of positive societal attitudes to people with disabilities, including children with SEN;
- the development of curricula which are suitable for meeting the needs of such pupils;
- the priority given to effective inclusion of such pupils within mainstream schools;
- the provision of adequate training for teachers working with pupils with SEN;
- the effective organisation and management of SEN provision in schools and LEAs.

Progress with each one of these factors has had an impact on the extent to which mainstream schools have been able to provide effectively for children with SEN (see Stakes and Hornby 1997).

Current practice for working with children with SEN is guided by several key documents. These include the legislation contained in the 1981 and 1996 Education Acts which embodied the philosophy of the Warnock Report; the 1988 Education Act which provided the framework for National Curriculum guidance; the Code of Practice for SEN which has provided the most extensive guidance to date; and the expectations set out in the OFSTED documentation on Frameworks for Inspection (OFSTED 1993). The implications of these key documents for mainstream school teachers are summarised after the following overview of the important issue of inclusion.

Inclusion

A major issue in mainstream school provision for pupils with SEN is the extent to which these pupils are actually included in such schools as opposed to being educated in special schools and classes. The 1981 Education Act reaffirmed the requirement of the 1976 Education Act regarding the desirability of including children with SEN within mainstream schools wherever possible. The 1981 Act indicated that the integration of children with special educational needs in mainstream schools should be dependent on whether the four criteria which were suggested by the Warnock Report could be met. These are that:

- inclusion in mainstream school is in accord with their parents' wishes;
- their educational needs can be met in the mainstream school;
- this is consistent with efficient use of resources; and
- their inclusion does not detract from the education of the other children.

The Green Paper on SEN (DfEE 1997a) takes a more forthright stance on inclusion and states:

> We support the UNESCO Salamanca World Statement on Special Needs Education (1994). This calls on Governments to adopt the principle of inclusive education, enrolling all children in regular schools unless there are compelling reasons for doing otherwise.

However, the Green Paper also emphasises that special schools and units will continue to be needed in order to provide for children whose SEN cannot be met in mainstream schools.

The Code of Practice for SEN, while making the point that the needs of most children with SEN can be met within mainstream schools, takes a moderate stance on inclusion by emphasising the importance of having a continuum of provision, from support within mainstream classrooms, through special units within mainstream schools, to separate special schools.

However, because of the increased emphasis on the inclusion of children with SEN in mainstream schools the number of these children is increasing, as are the severity and variety of their SEN. Children with a far wider range of learning difficulties and variety of medical conditions, as well as sensory difficulties and physical disabilities, are now attending mainstream classes. The implication of this is that mainstream school teachers need to expand their knowledge and skills with regard to the needs of children with SEN.

National Curriculum

Guidance on the National Curriculum (NC) for children with SEN suggests that they should follow this curriculum to the maximum extent possible (DES 1989). The NC stipulates that all children of school age are entitled to a 'broad and balanced' programme. The NC is a prescriptive programme which determines the majority of curriculum content for all children up to the age of sixteen. Children with a wide variety and severity of SEN are therefore to be provided for within this context.

Some children with SEN will have little difficulty in keeping pace with their peers while for others this will be a problem. For many children with SEN their curriculum programme will have to take into account not only their pace of learning but also the level they can cope with. In some situations the work of the teacher will necessarily focus on making the curriculum meaningful for their pupils, while for others it will serve a more radical purpose. Jordan (1991) for example, writing about the National Curriculum and children with autism, argues that the purpose of the National Curriculum should not be to confine children with SEN, rather it should be part of a broad and balanced total curriculum to meet their needs. What is the case for children with autism is arguably the same for children with profound and complex disabilities and in fact for all children with SEN.

OFSTED

OFSTED inspections focus on a range of issues regarding children with SEN. As a class-room teacher you need to be aware of their concern about standards of pupil achievement, the quality of learning and teaching, approaches to assessment, recording and reporting, planning and implementing the curriculum, pupil welfare and guidance, and links with parents.

When inspectors come into your classroom, they will pay particular attention to the relationship between work produced by children with SEN and the stated objectives of the lesson. They will also want to check whether pupils' achievements match the assessment of their ability. Inspectors will be looking for evidence that the standards achieved match the individual targets set for each pupil. They will also be looking at the quality of the pupil's past work in order to evaluate their progress.

Regarding *quality of pupil learning*, both learning skills and outcomes will be observed. Concerning learning skills, inspectors will assess whether pupils have a positive attitude to work and whether they pay sufficient attention in lessons. They will be looking to see if pupils remain involved with their work during the lesson and if they are able to participate fully and appropriately. Pupils' learning styles will also be considered, to see whether they are able to work collaboratively or independently when necessary and to what extent they are able to take responsibility for their own learning. Furthermore, inspectors will be assessing the degree to which pupils are able and willing to evaluate the quality of their work. For learning outcomes, inspectors will consider whether pupils achieve the required objectives and can apply the knowledge and skills they have learned in new situations.

For *quality of teaching* the inspectors are interested in how you have planned your lessons, particularly their content, appropriateness and relevance to the needs of all pupils in the class. They will want evidence that lessons are carefully planned to take account of the needs of pupils with SEN. Lesson plans should also show how you have incorporated the contributions of other professionals where appropriate. With respect to the teaching strategies you have selected, the inspectors will assess the teaching methods that are used to deliver the work you have planned. They will want to see variety in opportunities for pupils to learn, as well as appropriateness and effectiveness. Inspectors will want to see that the work set is sufficiently challenging for all pupils, while ensuring that its pace is appropriate. It is important to ensure that expectations for the outcomes of learning tasks are also appropriate and that there are positive interactions between yourself and pupils with SEN.

Assessment of pupils, *recording and reporting* will also be inspected. The focus on assessment involves checking your knowledge of a child's difficulties or disability and your awareness of the most up-to-date information that is available in school. They will also want to check on how you use this information in planning your lessons. Inspectors will also want to ensure that records for pupils with SEN follow school policy. Reports on pupils with SEN should celebrate their achievements, including achievements in personal and social education and vocational education, as well as conforming to whole-school reporting policy.

The focus of the inspection on the *curriculum* will be in assessing whether the programme provided for pupils with SEN is broad, balanced and relevant to their needs, that there are individual programmes of work in operation and all pupils enjoy equal access to the whole curriculum.

The inspection of pupils' *welfare and guidance* will focus on a review of the arrangements for the identification and support of pupils with emotional or behavioural difficulties. They will also wish to discover to what extent pupils with SEN are integrated into general class groupings for pastoral and curriculum support.

In the inspection of *links with parents*, inspectors will be assessing the extent to which parents are involved in decisions about the provision made to meet their child's needs. They may, for example, wish to enquire about your links with parents of children with SEN in your class. The extent of the child's involvement in such decisions will also be considered.

Code of Practice

The Code of Practice (DfE 1994a) is described as 'a guide for schools and LEAs about the practical help they can give to pupils with special educational needs' (p. 11). It makes recommendations as to how schools might encourage the development of good practice in both the organisation of provision for children with SEN and the delivery of the curriculum for them. It is the responsibility of all teachers to be aware of the requirements of the Code in detail. In this respect it is important that they should read it and discuss it with colleagues. Copies of the Revised Code will be available from the DfEE in 2001. However, since the Code is a complex document it may also be useful to read one of a variety of handbooks which have been prepared to help teachers interpret the Code (e.g. Hornby *et al.* 1995). A brief summary of the main features of the Code are outlined below.

The Code sets out a staged approach to meeting SEN, detailing the requirements for all involved in schools. It includes the responsibilities of all who work in schools, the governing body, and those with responsibilities for pupils with SEN in the LEA.

The Code details procedures for identifying, assessing and planning programmes to address pupils' SEN. This book focuses on the responsibilities of class teachers operating at the school-based stages of this process. At these stages the teacher's responsibility is to identify children with SEN and liaise with the school's Special Educational Needs Coordinator (SENCO) and others, in order to assess the child's needs and to develop plans to meet these needs. Teachers are also involved in reviewing children's progress. Unsatisfactory progress could lead to the child progressing through the various other stages which, for a minority of children, will result in a Statement of Special Educational Need being drawn up for them.

For children of school age the practices and procedures outlined in the Code are under-pinned by three key concepts. These are: a continuum of SEN; provision set in a broad, balanced and relevant curriculum; and a good working partnership with parents.

The continuum of need was a concept detailed in the Warnock Report relating to the wide range of difficulties which children experience. These range from mild, through to moderate to severe, and profound learning difficulties; and can range at one end to those pupils with SEN who are fully integrated within the mainstream school and who partici-pate fully in the activities offered, to those who are at the other end, who are taught outside the school system.

The curricular programme which is offered to pupils with SEN must be set within the National Curriculum and be taught at an appropriate level and pace. For many, particu-larly those with learning difficulties, these will be considerably lower than for many of their peers.

The partnership with parents of children with SEN is important for a number of reasons. Often, because their children have SEN they will need extra support and guidance. Furthermore, they will have information and experiences of their children from outside school which can provide a valuable perspective on their development within it. Parents also have a legal right to be informed of the progress of their children in school. Chapter 12 of this book is devoted to working with parents of children with SEN.

The majority of pupils in mainstream schools will be at the school-based stages of the Code. A few children with more severe or complex SEN will need to be catered for at the more advanced stages of the process which involve support and assessment from LEA specialists, and which for some will lead to Statements of special educational needs. The school-based stages focus on policy and provision established within schools, with contributions from teaching staff, the head teacher and the governing body.

Responsibilities of the class teacher

For the class teacher of children with SEN at the school-based stages there are several responsibilities. These include:

- the identification, as early as possible, of children likely to have special educational needs;
- making immediate provision for the teaching and assessment of these pupils;
- informing parents of decisions affecting their child, and developing a partnership for assessing and planning;
- informing and assisting the school SENCO to collect relevant information about children with SEN.

Other information which is useful in the identification and assessment of pupils with SEN includes:

- all current and past records relating to the child, including those from other schools they have attended;
- available data from any National Curriculum assessments;
- standardised test results, profiles of attainment or screening test results;
- information contained on records of achievement;
- school-based reports from teachers or others who have had contact with the child;
- observations of the child's behaviour;
- information on health or social problems which are known to the school.

Parents can provide additional information with regard to their child's health, behaviour and general development, which is relevant to their progress. They should also be asked for their views of the child's progress both at home and at school. Information may also be obtained from other agencies such as the health or social services which may have been involved, as well as from the children themselves.

The views of children should also be taken into consideration at all stages of the process. Specifically this relates to the children's perceptions of their difficulties and how they would like them to be addressed.

Individual Education Plans

Part of the processes identified in the Code of Practice relate to the use of Individual Education Plans (IEPs) with some pupils. The Code of Practice (p. 28) details seven areas that must be addressed in IEPs. These are:

- the nature of the child's learning difficulties;
- staff and programmes involved;
- parental involvement;
- targets to be achieved in specified time;
- pastoral or medical requirements;
- arrangements for monitoring and assessment;
- arrangements for review, including date.

The most important function of IEPs is the setting of specific learning targets for individual children over a predetermined period of time. For certain children there will be a whole series of targets across the curriculum on a rolling programme. The SENCO (or the member of staff given responsibility for this) sets the time when each IEP will be reviewed.

Each IEP review will consider the progress made and the strategies used. In setting new targets the strategies to achieve these should also be discussed as should approaches to assessing and monitoring further progress.

The overall responsibility for the coordination of these plans lies with the SENCO. However, the responsibility for determining the targets and the strategies to be used to teach and monitor progress in many lessons lies with the classroom teacher. For those with little experience in this area the situation may appear daunting. In practice the SENCO can provide help and guidance and should be approached if this is needed. Help may also be available if the child has an LEA learning support teacher who visits on a regular basis. However, this will only be the case if the child has triggered concerns which have led to the third stage outlined in the new Code of Practice.

Statements of Special Educational Need

Most pupils in special schools in England and Wales are subject to a Statement of Special Educational Need, and some pupils in mainstream schools have them. This is a legally binding document detailing the required educational provision for the pupil as well as the difficulties which the child has. It is determined by the recommendations of interested parties, with contributions from the school, the child's parents, representatives from the local services such as the school psychological service and social services; as well as representation from the LEA. Statements are reviewed annually so that the changing needs and circumstances of children can be taken into account.

The number of pupils with Statements varies widely from school to school. The 1980s saw a rise in the number of pupils placed in special schools. However, since then there has been a gradual fall in the numbers placed there (Audit Commission/HMI 1992). This has been matched by a corresponding rise in the number of pupils with Statements in mainstream schools during this period.

The Audit Commission/HMI Report also highlighted the considerable variation between the number of pupils with statements in different Local Educational Authorities. The percentage of the total school population with Statements varied between 3.2 and 0.8 per cent in a different LEA – a significant difference. This was put down to a lack of clarity of definition of special educational needs by LEAs. For others, such as Mortimore and Blackstone (1983) and Booth *et al.* (1992), social differences and variances in the value placed by parents on formal education were also regarded as important factors.

Types of SEN

The Code of Practice refers to eight different types of special educational need. These are listed below along with an additional category of 'gifted' or 'highly able' children, many of whom are considered to have SEN.

Learning difficulties
Children with learning difficulties have difficulties which range from *mild*, through *moderate* and *severe*, to *profound* and include those with *multiple* learning difficulties. Their difficulties in learning range from problems in acquiring basic literacy skills to problems in learning basic self-help skills such as dressing and toileting (see Chapter 2).

Specific learning difficulties
Children with *specific learning difficulties* have problems in acquiring basic literacy or numeracy skills in contrast to their abilities in other areas (see Chapter 2).

Gifted
Children of *high ability* are those whose learning potential is well above the average but whose academic achievements may not be commensurate with their ability, so they may be *gifted* underachievers (see Chapter 2).

Hearing difficulties
Children with *hearing difficulties* have levels of hearing loss ranging from mild and moderate to severe and profound (see Chapter 3).

Visual difficulties
Children with *visual difficulties* exhibit a wide range of visual losses, from those whose impairment is corrected by glasses to those who are blind (see Chapter 3).

Physical disabilities
Children with *physical disabilities* include those whose disability has resulted from a congenital condition such as cerebral palsy and others who have suffered an injury which has led to mobility problems (see Chapter 4).

Medical conditions
Children with *medical conditions* such as epilepsy or asthma may have associated SEN (see Chapter 4).

Speech and language difficulties
Children with *speech and language difficulties* exhibit a range of levels and types of communication problems (see Chapter 4).

Emotional and behavioural difficulties
Children with *emotional or behavioural difficulties* exhibit behaviours which make it difficult for them to function effectively at school, or they disrupt the education of other pupils (see Chapter 5).

Prevalence of SEN

Given the above broad definition of special educational needs, it is clear that all teachers will have some children with SEN in their classes. Of course some schools will have far more pupils with SEN than others but all schools will have a sizeable proportion of these pupils.

Estimates of the proportion of the entire school population who have SEN vary depending on the precise definition used and on the demands of the society in which the child is living. It is important to understand that what is considered to be a disability in one culture may not be in another. For example, consider a child with a club foot and another with dyslexia. In the UK the child with dyslexia is likely to experience major problems in school and later life whereas the one with a club foot will encounter relatively fewer difficulties. In contrast, a child with a club foot born into the Masai tribe in Africa will be severely handicapped by the inability to perform tribal dances, whereas the one with dyslexia will experience little difficulty since literacy is not important in that culture. Therefore, estimates of the prevalence of SEN are dependent on the impairments considered to be significantly disabling in each society.

Figures reported in the Warnock Report in 1978 suggested that around 20 per cent of pupils in schools would need, at some time during their schooling, some form of extra provision to meet their special educational needs. The Audit Commission/HMI Report (1992) indicated that the majority of pupils with SEN were already being catered for within ordinary schools, while around 0.8 per cent received extra help from their LEA or attended a unit within mainstream schools, and about 1.3 per cent of pupils attended a separate form of special provision such as special schools.

Identifying difficulties

The most important role of teachers at the primary school level is to identify children who are experiencing difficulties at school. Identification of such difficulties is the vital first step to finding out whether there is an SEN or not, and if there is, beginning to remedy this. For some pupils with physical or sensory difficulties the nature of the problem is clearly recognisable. A difficulty with movement is an example of this, as is a child who comes to school wearing glasses or another who wears a hearing aid. However, this will not always be the case and it may not be obvious to the teacher that the child has a disability. Without this information teachers will not always be aware that they may have to make adjustments to accommodate the needs of the child.

Learning difficulties are typically not as easy to recognise as physical or sensory disabilities. Often there are no outward signs to alert the teacher. Children with learning difficulties may seem, superficially at least, no different from other pupils and often give the teacher no clues as to why they are experiencing problems. The only obvious feature is that the child is unable to perform certain tasks set by the teacher as adequately as others in the class. The probable reasons need to be investigated in order to determine the nature and severity of the child's SEN.

The following four chapters provide guidelines for identifying the different types of SEN found in mainstream schools as well as some strategies which teachers can use to meet the needs of such pupils in mainstream schools.

Further reading

DfE (1994) *Code of Practice on the Identification and Assessment of Special Educational Needs*. London: Central Office of Information.

Hornby, G., Davis, G. and Taylor, G. (1995) *The Special Educational Needs Coordinator's Handbook: Guidelines for Implementing the Code of Practice*. London: Routledge.

Stakes, J. R. and Hornby, G. (1997) *Change in Special Education: What Brings it about?* London: Cassell.

Tilstone, C. *et al.* (1999) *Pupils with Learning Difficulties in Mainstream Schools*. London: David Fulton Publishers.

Tod, J., Castle, F. and Blamires, M. (1998) *IEPs: Implementing Effective Practice*. London: David Fulton Publishers.

CHAPTER 2

Children with differing abilities

Introduction

This chapter focuses on children whose cognitive abilities differ from the norm in some way or other. These include children with difficulties in all aspects of learning, such as those with severe learning difficulties, and children with atypical patterns of learning, such as those with autism. It also includes those with learning difficulties in specific areas, such as dyslexic children as well as those with high ability and often referred to as gifted.

Learning difficulties

Children with learning difficulties make up the largest group of children with SEN. Learning difficulties range from *mild*, through *moderate* and *severe*, to *profound* and *multiple* learning difficulties. Children with severe, profound and multiple learning difficulties are small in number compared with those who have mild or moderate learning difficulties who make up the majority of this group. Children are identified as having *mild learning difficulties* if they are experiencing problems in acquiring basic literacy and numeracy skills. Children with *moderate learning difficulties* are, in addition, likely to have delayed speech and language development, poor social skills and also may exhibit emotional or behavioural difficulties. Children with *severe learning difficulties* are likely to have substantial problems in all these areas as well as possible problems in learning basic self-help skills such as dressing and toileting. Children with *profound* or *multiple learning difficulties* will have major problems in acquiring all of the above skills.

The vast majority of children with mild learning difficulties are found in mainstream classes. In the past, a large proportion of children with moderate learning difficulties were placed in special schools but increasingly these pupils are being educated in mainstream schools in either special units or mainstream classrooms. The majority of children with severe learning difficulties and those with profound or multiple learning difficulties are placed in special schools. However, many special schools have links with mainstream schools which enable an increasing number of these children to spend some of their time in ordinary schools.

Distribution of abilities

This chapter focuses on those children whose cognitive or intellectual abilities differ from the norm in some way or other. Cognitive ability is one of the most important variables determining children's ability to learn and achieve well academically. Measures of cognitive ability are therefore considered to be useful predictors of children's learning potential. The best known measures of cognitive ability are tests of intellectual ability or IQ tests. It is now realised that because cultural and environmental factors affect scores on IQ tests these cannot be regarded as fixed. However, they do provide a useful prediction of learning potential, especially where IQ scores vary markedly from the norm. Therefore, the next section will use the concept of IQ scores to illustrate how children's abilities differ within a typical school population.

If all school children in the country at a particular age were given an IQ test and their scores plotted on a graph, the graph obtained would be the shape of a bell-shaped curve, which is often referred to as a normal distribution. Since IQ tests are usually constructed so that they have an average score of 100 and a standard deviation of 15 points, the statistical properties of the normal distribution can be used to work out the proportion of children whose IQ scores fall either within the average range or outside it. This is illustrated in Figure 2.1.

It is clear from Figure 2.1 that around 68 per cent of the children's IQ scores will fall within the average range, which is from 85 to 115 points. Thus, around two thirds of children are considered to have intellectual ability within the average range. Another 13.5 per cent of children have IQs between 115 and 130 so are considered to have above average intelligence. A further 2.5 per cent have IQs above 130 so are considered to be of high ability and may be referred to as gifted. This means that altogether 84 per cent of children have either average or above average IQ scores and therefore should have sufficient intellectual ability to be able to cope with the demands of mainstream schooling. However, this also

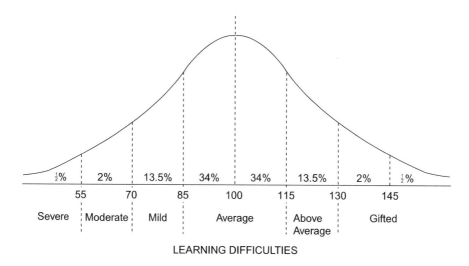

Figure 2.1 Normal distribution of IQ scores

means that 16 per cent of children have below average IQ scores and intellectual ability and are therefore likely to have difficulty coping with the demands of regular schooling.

Of the children with below average IQ scores, 2.5 per cent have IQs below 70. These are children with moderate, severe or profound learning difficulties, many of whom are educated in special schools or units. This is especially the case for those children with severe or profound learning difficulties (together referred to as SLD) whose IQ scores are below 50 points. However, the trend is for an increasing proportion of these children to attend mainstream schools, particularly those with moderate learning difficulties (MLD) who have IQs between approximately 50 and 75 points. The remaining 13.5 per cent have IQs between approximately 70 and 85 points. These are children with mild learning difficulties who, in the past, were sometimes referred to as slow learners. All of these children are educated in mainstream schools and make up three or four members of the typical primary school class.

Children with mild and moderate learning difficulties therefore make up a large proportion of the students with SEN in primary schools and an even larger proportion of students in some secondary schools. These are the pupils who are likely to have difficulty in learning basic reading, writing and number skills. They will need extra help in order to develop the 3Rs. Even given this additional help most of them are unlikely to be able to do well in examinations such as the GCSE at age 16 years. Therefore, the goals of education for these pupils need to be somewhat different. Different teaching approaches and different curricula are needed, particularly for pupils with MLD in the secondary school. In the primary school, teaching should be adapted so that these pupils are encouraged to develop the highest levels of oracy, literacy and numeracy of which they are capable. In the secondary school, curricula for these pupils need to be more vocationally than academically orientated, with emphasis placed on the development of life skills.

When pupils with mild and moderate learning difficulties are provided with appropriate education they can be successful in adult life. Many of them obtain jobs as skilled or semi-skilled workers and are considered excellent employees. However, many pupils with such learning difficulties who have not received an appropriate education typically leave school with no examination certificates, few skills and low self-esteem. It is not surprising that many of them feel failures and find it difficult to be successful in adult life.

It is therefore of crucial importance that these pupils are not considered to be unable to learn just because they have difficulties in learning the 3Rs. They can learn and do very well in adult life when suitable curricula and teaching approaches are employed. Examples of these are outlined in the following sections for children with mild, moderate and severe learning difficulties and in subsequent sections for the other types of SEN.

Mild learning difficulties

These children have below average intellectual ability with IQ scores of around 70 to 85 points. They are the largest group of children with SEN but because of the mild nature of their SEN are typically not identified until during their primary schooling. The vast majority of these children are educated in mainstream schools.

Signs to help in identifying this type of SEN
- they may have a short attention span;
- they may have difficulty understanding instructions;
- they are slow to learn reading, writing and number skills;
- they tend to develop behavioural difficulties.

Strategies for teaching these children
- focus on the child's strengths as well as weaknesses;
- start from what the child knows and go at the pace of the child;
- ensure tasks are within the child's capacity in order to ensure success;
- use semantic/concept mapping to build on the child's existing knowledge;
- include lots of repetition, praise and encouragement;
- use range of resource materials – visual aids such as charts/artefacts;
- use peer tutoring and cooperative learning groups;
- give access to computer for drill, skill building and word processing;
- work closely with parents, other teachers and specialists;
- use self-esteem/confidence building exercises.

Moderate learning difficulties

These children have below average intellectual ability with IQ scores of around 50 to 70 or 75 points. They are typically not identified until the early years of primary schooling. Many of these children are educated in ordinary schools with some in special schools or units.

Signs to help in identifying this type of SEN
- they have a short attention span;
- they have difficulty understanding instructions;
- they are slow to learn reading, writing and number skills;
- they tend to be immature and have behavioural difficulties;
- they tend to have delayed speech and language skills.

Strategies for teaching these children
- focus on the child's strengths as well as weaknesses;
- start from what the child knows and go at the pace of the child;
- ensure tasks are within the child's capacity in order to ensure success;
- use semantic/concept mapping to build on the child's existing knowledge;
- include lots of repetition, praise and encouragement;
- focus on oral language and social skills such as following directions;
- use practical activities – games, simulations, role-plays and field trips;
- use range of resource materials – visual aids such as charts/artefacts;
- use peer tutoring and cooperative learning groups;
- give access to computer for drill, skill building and word processing;

- work closely with parents, other teachers and specialists;
- participate fully in IEP meetings and set suitable targets;
- use self-esteem/confidence building exercises.

Severe learning difficulties

These children have well below average intellectual ability with IQ scores of below 50 points. They have learning difficulties in most aspects of life. They are typically identified during their preschool years. Most of them are educated in special schools or units in mainstream schools but an increasing number of them are attending mainstream schools, particularly in the early years of primary schooling.

Signs to help in identifying this type of SEN
- they are slow to begin to walk *and* talk;
- their speech is not clear and their vocabulary is limited;
- they have poor fine and gross coordination skills;
- they have great difficulties learning reading, writing and number skills;
- their behaviour is immature; prefer to be with adults or young children.

Strategies for teaching these children
- focus on the child's strengths as well as weaknesses;
- start from what the child knows and go at a manageable pace;
- break tasks down into small steps, teaching one step at a time;
- focus on developing oral language and daily living skills;
- work on social skills such as making friends or asking for help;
- ensure tasks are within the child's capacity in order to ensure success;
- use practical/concrete/hands-on activities such as counting money;
- include lots of repetition, praise and encouragement;
- work closely with parents, other teachers and specialists;
- participate in Individualised Educational Planning meetings at school;
- decide on priorities – what the child must, should and could learn;
- focus on the child's happiness, confidence and self-esteem.

Autistic children

These children have difficulties with most aspects of life but also have certain features which distinguish them from children with other types of learning difficulties. Most of them are educated in special schools or units but an increasing number are attending mainstream schools.

Signs to help in identifying this type of SEN
- very delayed speech and language development; may echo words or phrases;
- lack of interest in relating to others, including their parents;

- repetitive or stereotyped behaviour such as rocking or head banging;
- insistence on routines; angry outbursts when these are disrupted;
- obsessive interest in certain objects; spin small objects or self;
- either no response or over-sensitivity to sound.

Strategies for teaching these children
- ensure you have the child's attention before giving instructions;
- start from what the child knows and go at the pace of the child;
- break tasks down into small steps, teaching one step at a time;
- use level of language appropriate for the child, accompanied by appropriate gestures;
- focus on oral language and daily living skills;
- work on social skills such as eye contact and asking for something;
- give enough information for the child to complete tasks as independently as possible;
- present the material in an organised manner, not too much at one time;
- present appropriate level of prompts, ideally before the child responds incorrectly;
- include lots of repetition, praise and encouragement;
- provide the child with clear feedback with regard to their behaviour and work;
- reward desirable behaviour; withdraw privileges for misbehaviour;
- ignore annoying behaviour; use 'time out' for disruptive behaviour;
- work closely with parents, other teachers and specialists;
- participate in Individualised Educational Planning meetings at school;
- decide priorities for what the child needs to learn;
- focus on the child's happiness, confidence and self-esteem.

Specific learning difficulty (Dyslexia)

Dyslexic children have specific learning difficulties in the areas of spelling, writing, reading and/or mathematics but can function well in other aspects of the curriculum. The vast majority of children with specific learning difficulties are educated in mainstream class-rooms.

Signs to help in identifying this type of SEN
- discrepancy between the child's oral language skills and written work;
- difficulties with auditory or visual skills/short-term memory/sequencing;
- problems with concentration, organisation, or left–right orientation.

Strategies for teaching these children
- find out the child's strengths, such as sport or art, and encourage these;
- emphasise oral/practical approaches, e.g. semantic mapping;
- sit the child towards the front of the class and minimise copying from board;
- select material to match the child's reading level and interests;
- break tasks into small steps and allow adequate time for completion;
- select and highlight most important spelling errors, not all of them;

- get the child to use 'look, say, cover, write, say, check' to learn spellings;
- use audio/visual aids such as video/audio recorder or language master;
- get the child to use a word processor with spell-checker as much as possible;
- teach study skills, e.g. mnemonics; Survey, Question, Read, Recite, Review;
- facilitate phonological awareness through rhymes, listening exercises, etc.;
- use buddy systems, peer tutoring and cooperative learning within class;
- give lots of praise and encouragement and maintain high expectations;
- involve parents in reinforcing school programme at home;
- work on the child's happiness, confidence and self-esteem.

Gifted or high ability children

Gifted students are those with well above average intellectual ability. They are not part of the SEN Code of Practice but may have special needs related to underachievement. For example, some of them may be performing at average levels in school subjects despite having learning potential which is well above the average. Teachers will find the procedures embodied in the Code useful in providing an optimum education for pupils who are gifted but are underachieving, in the same way that these procedures are useful for pupils with SEN.

Signs to help in identification
- pupil finds work easy and finishes it quickly;
- is observant and curious;
- demonstrates surprising knowledge or insight;
- can think abstractly;
- shows high level of argument and problem-solving skills.

Strategies for teaching these children
- ensure pace of work required is suitable – not too slow, not too fast;
- seek to extend the child's knowledge rather than rush through syllabus;
- use questioning to probe for deeper understanding;
- use concept mapping to develop conceptual understanding;
- set tasks which have different levels/progression of difficulty;
- increase challenge level of some tasks set, e.g. some homework tasks;
- select high ability groups to work on extension activities;
- use cooperative learning/peer tutoring to develop helping/social skills;
- encourage development of study skills and self-directed learning;
- organise enrichment activities such as field trips/competitions;
- organise senior students or staff to act as mentors;
- promote class and school ethos in which high ability is valued;
- encourage involvement in extracurricular activities and clubs;
- encourage all-round development, focus on strengths and weaknesses;
- work closely with parents to ensure a consistent approach.

Further guidance about these types of SEN is available from:

- the school's SENCO;
- educational psychologists;
- LEA advisers, education Officers for SEN;
- Special School or Special Unit teachers;
- Associations for gifted children, those with dyslexia, children with learning difficulties, e.g. MENCAP. (A list of addresses of some of the Associations that provide advice for teachers is included at the end of this book.)

Further reading

Eyre, D. (1997) *Able Children in Ordinary Schools.* London: David Fulton Publishers.

Jordan, R. and Jones, G. (1999) *Meeting the Needs of Children with Autistic Spectrum Disorders.* London: David Fulton Publishers.

Tilstone, C. (1991) *Teaching Children with Severe Learning Difficulties.* London: David Fulton Publishers.

Walton, M. (1998) *Teaching Reading and Spelling to Dyslexic Children.* London: David Fulton Publishers.

CHAPTER 3

Children with hearing and visual difficulties

Introduction

This chapter concentrates on the difficulties of children who have either visual or hearing impairments. It considers problems such as how these manifest themselves, what difficulties can occur in the learning situation and what approaches are most successful for the classroom teacher to employ in order to minimise these.

Increasingly, since the 1981 Education Act, there has been a move towards greater integration of pupils with both sight and hearing difficulties into mainstream schools. The children who have been integrated have a wide range of impairments from relatively mild problems, which may mean that they must sit in a particular part of the room to gain most benefit from their lessons, to those pupils who have considerably greater problems and need the help of specialist teachers and equipment.

There are important consequences for the class teacher when a child with sight problems or a hearing loss is in the classroom and it is important that the consequences for the class teacher are discussed. Of course, specialist advice should be obtainable from the SENCO, but some basic information about the issues raised by these impairments is essential for good management by the class teacher.

Hearing difficulties

Manifestations
Children with hearing difficulties make up probably the second largest group of children with SEN, after those with learning difficulties. Levels of hearing impairment range from mild and moderate to severe and profound. Children with mild or moderate losses are the most numerous and are typically placed in mainstream classes. Those with severe and profound losses tend to be placed in units in mainstream schools or in special schools. Children with all levels of hearing difficulties are at risk of experiencing problems in learning basic literacy and numeracy skills and may become withdrawn or disruptive in school.

There are two types of hearing loss: conductive and sensorineural. The first of these is often caused by a blockage in the ear like wax or 'glue ear' which results from a collection of fluid in the ear when a child has catarrh or a heavy cold. These cases are often treatable medically and hearing can be restored, often to within normal limits. Many young children suffer from these problems, which are often accompanied by poor speech, limited vocabulary, poor comprehension of spoken language and difficulties in discriminating and sequencing sounds, as well as problems in listening.

Sensorineural hearing losses are generally caused by difficulties with the nerves which link to the ear. These are more serious, usually irreversible. Typically a hearing aid is needed to produce amplification of sound but it is important to realise that this will not restore normal hearing. Depending on the level of loss, a hearing aid will help children to discriminate sounds. This will be distorted, however. The number of pupils suffering from this type of difficulty is very small. Figures mentioned by Sherliker (1994) indicate that only some 0.1 per cent of pupils are in this category.

Effects of conductive hearing loss
When this type of hearing loss arises children may:

- find listening difficult;
- be slow in learning to talk;
- have unclear speech;
- feel insecure and confused in class;
- not hear clearly in a noisy classroom;
- be withdrawn and often wait for cues from other children;
- give the impression of being able to listen on occasions.

Effects of sensorineural hearing loss
With this type of hearing loss most pupils will have difficulty with the higher frequencies of sound used in speech and what they will hear will be unpredictable. In these cases it is important to check what the child has heard. They can have particular difficulties with the more complex structures in the language and, of course, this will affect their overall understanding.

Strategies to help pupils with hearing losses
Webster and Elwood (1985) and Webster and Wood (1989) provide useful information for those working with pupils with hearing difficulties. They suggest that the following are of importance:

- the use of visual clues to make it clear what is being said;
- emphasis of the important instructions or key words;
- preparing children for the introduction of a new topic;
- allowing children time to find out about the topic in advance;
- writing new vocabulary on the whiteboard/flipchart;
- giving homework instructions when the class is quiet;
- allowing a friend to check that the instructions and information are clear;
- rephrasing as well as repeating phrases and words not understood;

- in oral lessons making sure the pace of discussion is not too fast;
- when other children answer questions repeating their answers;
- making sure children can see the teacher's face when they need to listen;
- not walking about the room when giving instructions;
- keeping classroom noise as low as possible;
- avoiding giving notes to the class orally;
- adapting outdoor activities to ensure full participation and safety.

Visual difficulties

Manifestations
Visual skills, as with hearing skills, are important in so many ways in the learning process. For children with sight problems there can be difficulties in learning to read, in itself a critical factor in success at school. This section outlines these problems and discusses some of the strategies which are available to help alleviate them.

Children with visual difficulties make up the smallest group of children with SEN. There is a wide range of levels of visual difficulty and also several differing forms of visual impairment, each with different implications for the child's education. A small proportion of this group are totally blind and are mostly educated in special schools or units within ordinary schools. However, the vast majority of children with visual difficulties have what is termed partial sight or low vision and are found in mainstream classes or special units within mainstream schools.

Some mild visual difficulties may not be identified until the early years of primary schooling, or even later. By the time children reach secondary school age most of those who have problems will have been discovered and some form of remedial action taken. As with hearing difficulties, the remedies can vary according to the level of impairment. Teachers should be aware that for some pupils with relatively severe problems special arrangements need to be made, such as the use of a brailler for a blind student or a closed-circuit TV for a student with low vision. Normally the school will be aware of those pupils in this category and the SENCO will inform the rest of the staff in the school.

What to look out for
Chapman and Stone (1988) and Best (1992) indicated that children with sight problems may display a number of characteristics. These include:

- clumsiness;
- poor hand–eye coordination;
- holding the head in an unusual way;
- frowning, making faces, or squinting more often than normal;
- often complaining of headaches or dizziness;
- having poorly formed handwriting;
- having difficulty in seeing the whiteboard/flipchart;
- becoming tired more quickly than other children.

If children display a number of these characteristics it is worth checking with someone else in the school to see if there is a recognised sight problem. For a variety of reasons children might be reluctant to wear glasses and attempt to hide their difficulties. If a problem is suspected this is an aspect worth checking.

Strategies to help pupils with visual difficulties
It is worth making a number of points here relating both to teaching technique and to classroom organisation. It is common practice for a teacher to move around the classroom during a lesson. There are strong disciplinary reasons for doing this. However, for those pupils with sight difficulties this movement can be very distracting and a teacher may need to consciously limit the amount of movement to that which is essential.

Similarly, children with difficulties in this area can have problems with the number of visual stimuli that they have to deal with in a lesson. Constant eye movement between the whiteboard, the teacher, a textbook or an exercise book may cause severe difficulties. Teachers should bear this in mind and try to plan lessons accordingly.

Vision is used by us all as a major learning tool. For those pupils with sight problems this can be a slower process than for the rest of us. They may for example, not be able to see the detail that children with good sight are able to, or perhaps they may take longer to assimilate information. Again, a note should be made of this and allowances made for such pupils.

As has already been mentioned, reading can cause problems for children with visual difficulties. Sometimes it is necessary to increase the size of the print in a book or photocopied worksheet to enable them to see more easily. For others, it is the paper that is used which causes the difficulties: in these cases matt white paper can be better to read from than glossy paper, which reflects light.

Poor formation of letters when completing written work is a possible sign of sight problems. This can be compounded by poor hand–eye coordination. For some children a sloping surface can help them to develop their skills. Time may also be needed to allow the child to experiment with the tool best suited for writing, the size of the lines on the paper, as well as finding the best position in the classroom for seeing the whiteboard. Where circumstances allow, children with visual difficulties can benefit from the lesson being taped so that they can listen to it later and absorb the information at their own speed.

Careful, clear labelling of materials and displays in the classroom can help visually impaired pupils. Similarly, corridors, and the aisles between desks and tables, that are free of obstructions, are essential for easy movement by these pupils.

Both sunlight and artificial lighting can cause problems in certain circumstances. The problem will vary according to the type of visual loss, and advice needs to be sought on this issue from specialist teachers to develop the best approach for each individual pupil.

For children with certain difficulties there is a need for them to use typewriters and computer facilities rather than a pen or pencil. This has created problems in the past because of the extra noise that such machines make in the classroom. Modern technology has certainly helped to reduce this to a large extent and has helped in both the production of high quality presentation and variable large size print for children to read more easily.

However, the pace at which they can use the machinery remains problematic for some children and consideration needs to be given to extra time to complete work.

The following is a summary of strategies which can be used for teaching children with visual difficulties:

- find out from parents/specialists exactly what the child's difficulties are;
- encourage the child to use visual aids prescribed, e.g. glasses, magnifiers;
- seat the child appropriately in the classroom, e.g. in the middle, towards the front;
- make sure the lighting is suitable; eliminate glare from the desk and whiteboard;
- use worksheets with correct print size, enlarged if necessary;
- ensure good contrast on any visual materials used – black and white is best;
- supplement visual information with verbal explanation;
- use concrete materials and hands-on experiences wherever possible;
- allow more time to complete tasks, and provide breaks to combat fatigue;
- arrange for other children to act as buddies, and use peer tutoring;
- do not lower expectations because the student has visual impairment.

Further reading

Arter, C., *et al.* (1999) *Children with Visual Impairment in Mainstream Settings.* London: David Fulton Publishers.

Best, A. B. (1992) *Teaching Children with Visual Impairments.* Milton Keynes: Open University Press.

Watson, L., Gregory, S. and Powers, S. (1999) *Deaf and Hearing Impaired Pupils in Mainstream Schools.* London: David Fulton Publishers.

Webster, A. and Elwood, J. (1985) *The Hearing Impaired Child in the Ordinary School.* Beckenham: Croom Helm.

CHAPTER 4

Children with physical disabilities, medical conditions and communication difficulties

Introduction

For some children learning experiences will be affected by communication difficulties, physical disabilities or medical conditions. There is an increasing number of these pupils to be found in mainstream schools. In many cases, knowledge of the child's condition needs to be gained from parents, medical practitioners and, in some cases, other professionals concerned with them. A basic knowledge of the medical and physical conditions of children in their classes is essential to teachers, as is information on the educational implications.

Historically, pupils with major physical disabilities and medical difficulties were not generally catered for in mainstream schools. However, since the 1981 Education Act, this has changed. It is also the case that far more children with unusual medical conditions are to be found in mainstream schools. It is essential that class teachers are adequately prepared to meet the needs of these children. Teachers need to know what these conditions mean in terms of the children's active participation in the school, their mobility, and the arrangements which need to be made to accommodate these aspects. They also need a knowledge of strategies that can be used to facilitate the pupils' learning.

Children with *physical disabilities* make up one of the smaller groups of pupils with SEN. They include those whose disability has resulted from a congenital condition and others who have suffered an injury. Some physically disabled children, such as those with cerebral palsy or spina bifida, may also experience sensory and neurological impairments with consequent learning difficulties. Other children, whose physical disabilities have resulted from serious illnesses such as muscular dystrophy or cystic fibrosis, may experience emotional difficulties. Children who have severe learning difficulties in addition to a physical disability are typically placed in special schools. However, the majority of children who have only a physical disability are educated in mainstream schools.

Children with *medical conditions* may have associated SEN for several reasons. Children with conditions such as epilepsy or asthma may require drug treatment which impairs their concentration. Children with life-threatening conditions such as heart disease, cancer, brain tumours or cystic fibrosis may need frequent hospital treatment which necessitates considerable absences from school. Other chronic conditions such as diabetes, eczema and rheumatoid arthritis may deplete a child's reserves of energy. Thus, all these medical conditions can have a negative impact on children's academic attainment. In addition, the psychological impact of such conditions can lead to children experiencing emotional or behavioural difficulties.

Lansdown (1980) and Halliday (1989) identified and listed the most common physical disabilities and medical conditions which include asthma, brittle bone disease, cerebral palsy, cystic fibrosis, diabetes, epilepsy, muscular dystrophy, spina bifida and hydrocephalus. Other disabilities or conditions also considered below are aphasia, dyspraxia, autism, ADHD and Down's syndrome. Information on the educational implications of these conditions and the development of appropriate teaching strategies is the focus of the following sections. A later section of the chapter will consider the impact of communication difficulties.

Aphasia

Children who are aphasic have problems with spoken language and are unable to use it appropriately. They can suffer from acquired or developmental aphasia. Children with this medical condition can be placed on a continuum relative to their degree of difficulty. Children described as aphasic suffer from severe impairment, those with relatively fewer problems are described as dysphasic.

The most common causes of aphasia are brain damage or profound deafness. However, recent research has shown that aphasia can occur when neither of these circumstances pertain and is caused by a child's specific failure of the normal language functions. Children with this condition need specific help, often through a specialised language unit or a speech therapist. They may need particular help with organising and sequencing their work and need additional means of communication. Extra classroom support may also be necessary for them. Aphasia can lead to frustrations, which may make children aggressive or defensive, and they may therefore need extra help learning social and turn-taking skills in the classroom.

Asthma

Asthma is a common medical condition. Some four per cent of the population are asthmatic to a degree. However, a much smaller percentage have severe problems. If this is the case for some children in your school they may have periods of absence from school. They are also likely to be unable to participate fully in certain curricular activities. The educational implications are:

- the child may need to catch up on missed work;
- PE and games may be difficult to participate in fully and alternative activities may need to be found;
- cold or dry weather may be more problematic for the child;
- discussion with parents may be necessary to work out how best physical activities might be undertaken;
- food allergies need to be checked on;
- reminders may be necessary about the use of an inhaler.

In the event of an attack the basic rules are:

- keep the child calm;
- ensure that the appropriate emergency medication is taken;
- send for another member of staff;
- call for an ambulance if: the shortness of breath continues; or the child is unable to stand up or speak; or the child is turning blue or the pulse rate exceeds 120 per minute; or the attack lasts longer than 15 minutes after medication is taken.

Attention Deficit Hyperactivity Disorder

Attention Deficit Hyperactivity Disorder (ADHD) may or may not be regarded as a medical condition. This is dependent on individual circumstances and the agencies that have been involved in the diagnostic procedure. Where a member of the medical profession has been involved and medication prescribed, it is more likely that the condition will be regarded as medical, in contrast to where there has been no contact with the family GP or local hospital.

ADHD is a condition that affects up to ten per cent of all children. It is mainly a problem with boys. Boys are six times more likely to be referred than girls. It is thought that the true ratio is three to one, with a large number of girls remaining undiagnosed. Most children with ADHD come to light in their junior school years. It is usually a hereditary condition. Most sufferers have a close relative (usually male) who has been affected to some degree by the same problem. Most ADHD children have a social maturity of about two thirds their actual age. Sixty per cent of ADHD children will carry some of their difficult behaviour into adulthood. ADHD affects a similar proportion of children in every country across the world. Many parents of ADHD children feel inadequate and have feelings that in some way they are to blame for their child's behaviour.

ADHD refers to a cluster of consistent behaviours including impulsiveness, over-activity, inattention, insatiability, disorganisation and social clumsiness. ADHD is a chronic problem, affecting learning and behaviour, and, although its presentation may change, problems are likely to continue to cause difficulties throughout the school years. Inattention causes ADHD children to function poorly in school. Difficulties occur in completing work unless they are given one-to-one supervision.

Autism

Children with this condition exhibit what is commonly described as a 'triad of impairment'. This triad consists of delayed language development, bizarre behaviour and difficulties with social relationships. Children with autism have difficulties across all modes of communication: speech, intonation, gesture, facial expression and body language. Their thought processes are often rigid, ritualistic and obsessive. Changes in routine can be difficult, if not impossible, to accommodate. As a result, children with autism have difficulties with social relationships. They exhibit poor social timing in contact with others, a lack of empathy with those around them, a rejection of normal body contact and inappropriate eye contact.

Autism is a disability that is more commonly found in boys than girls. It is usually diagnosed before school age. Autism has no apparent physical features and therefore children with this difficulty may not be immediately recognisable. However, the difficulties of children with this condition do manifest themselves clearly as you get to know the child. Children with autistic difficulties have major communication problems that can cause them to be both immature and deviant. Difficulties with communication are often accompanied by bizarre behaviour. This can make the child difficult to deal with in the mainstream school classroom.

The most severe cases of children on the autistic spectrum will need specialist help, usually organised outside the mainstream school. However, increasingly more and more children on this spectrum are attending mainstream schools, particularly in their primary school years.

Children on the autistic spectrum can vary considerably in their overall ability. Some children have high intelligence, while others display particularly well developed skills in certain areas of the curriculum. These areas often include maths, music and art. The more able autistic child is often diagnosed as having Asperger's syndrome. It is these children who are most often placed in mainstream schools.

Jordan and Powell (1995) have argued for recognition of the importance of structured teaching for children on the autistic spectrum. They claim that teachers must structure their classroom in order to effectively teach children with this condition. This must include the physical layout of the room and the provision of a suitable framework for teaching through systematic and structured activities.

Suggested strategies for teaching children on the autistic spectrum were provided in Chapter 2.

Brittle bone disease

Pupils with brittle bone disease are no more likely to have learning difficulties than the rest of their peer group. They may, however, have difficulties with participation in games and PE and other physical activities. They may also need:

- time to catch up with work missed during periods of hospitalisation;
- aids for mobility;

- aids for writing;
- extra time for the completion of examinations and assessments;
- clutter removed from classrooms to lessen the risk of falling;
- positive intervention to aid emotional adjustment.

Cerebral palsy

Cerebral palsy is a condition caused by damage to the brain. There are three forms: spasticity (where movement is often stiff and jerky), athetosis (manifested through jerky and irregular movements) and ataxia (which produces difficulties with balance and coordination). As far as the education of children with this condition is concerned there are a variety of implications:

- mobility problems – some children will be ambulant, others will need wheelchairs;
- fine motor control may be affected, as may be visual perception;
- problems with speech articulation – for some children communication aids will be necessary;
- support and intervention from outside professionals will be needed;
- long periods of hospitalisation may be needed – extra teaching will be necessary when this is the case;
- some will have a negative self-image and will need much support.

Cystic fibrosis

Cystic fibrosis is an incurable genetic disorder. The secretion of abnormally thick mucus in the lungs and the pancreas results in obstructions or infections of the bronchial tube or the stomach. Children with this condition will require treatment daily. This may include breathing exercises, physiotherapy, courses of antibiotics and a high protein diet to aid digestion.

Children with this condition are no more likely to have learning difficulties than their peers. Any effects on the achievement of children with this condition are likely to have been caused by absence and hospitalisation. With care, they should be able to participate fully in the curriculum programme. However, certain specific allowances will need to be made. These might include:

- a room with privacy if postural drainage is necessary;
- longer time to eat their meals;
- the need to be excused PE on a regular basis;
- they regularly feel ill and need to have frequent absences from school.

Diabetes

Diabetes is caused through the breakdown of the production of insulin in the body. Children can often develop diabetes quite suddenly and then need dietary restrictions and, in more severe cases, the injection of insulin to control it. An imbalance of blood sugar in the body will make the child feel unwell. Too little glucose will result in headaches, paleness, sweating, shaking, confusion, fear, mood swings and in some cases result in a coma.

The education programme for children with diabetes should follow the normal course. The teacher will need to be aware of the above symptoms and be prepared with food or drink for the child to have during lessons. In some circumstances the child will be able to recognise when problems are starting and ask permission to eat in class. This should be granted.

School trips will need to be organised carefully to ensure there are opportunities for eating stops. If this is taken into account the child should be able to participate fully in all activities. A useful school pack is available from the British Diabetes Association.

Down's syndrome

Down's syndrome is a genetic disorder that affects all races and both genders. It has also been referred to as Mongolism and Trisomy 21. It is caused by a chromosome abnormality. Children with this condition have 47 chromosomes instead of the usual 46. The chance of Down's syndrome increases with the age of the mother and to a lesser extent the father. The incidence of Down's syndrome among mothers aged 30 is estimated to be around 1:800, while for mothers aged 44 it can be as high as 1:50.

Down's syndrome can be diagnosed before birth through various tests but none are a hundred per cent reliable. Specific physical characteristics are usually apparent at birth. Sometimes the physical characteristics are accompanied by medical abnormalities. Physically, the baby will have particular facial features. These include a small, round head, often flatter at the back. Often the hairline is lower than on other children. The nose will be small, with a flatter bridge than normal. This is because of a lack of development or absence of the nasal bone. They may also have abnormalities of the eyes such as cataracts, squints or nystagmus. The fingers will be short and stubby, with the little finger curved inwards. Often they will have deformed feet, with the big toe widely separated from the other toes. Often these children have short limbs, which makes their height on the low side of normal.

Physically, around 40 per cent of children with Down's syndrome suffer from heart disease. In childhood, respiratory diseases are common, and Down's children particularly suffer from bronchitis. Middle ear infections are also common and a majority have some degree of hearing loss. Many suffer from inflammation of the eyelids, as an enzyme is not present in their teardrops.

Children with Down's syndrome are often described as happy and affectionate. However, this is not the case for all this group of children, as some can display signs of behavioural difficulties. Their overall development is delayed, including their language and social skills which can lead to difficulties in many situations. They also exhibit difficulties with both gross and fine motor skills. Young children with this condition can have difficulties with toilet training. As a result of these problems, progress will be slow in a large number of areas. They may display a lack of confidence and have difficulties communicating with others around them.

In most cases a child with Down's syndrome in a mainstream school will have a Statement of Special Educational Needs and be accompanied by a learning support assistant. Just how many hours they will be allocated, and how these are best deployed, will depend on the severity of the condition. It is also essential that parental contact is made regularly. (For suggestions for teaching children with Down's syndrome see the section on severe learning difficulties in Chapter 2.)

Dyspraxia

Children with dyspraxia are unable to programme their speech muscles to produce sounds for acceptable speech. Dyspraxia is an increasingly common condition, estimated to affect between three and six per cent of the school population. It is also known as 'clumsy child syndrome' and can affect other muscles in the body, leading to poor motor control. This can affect a child's ability to write neatly, play sport or a musical instrument or even tie up their shoelaces.

Epilepsy

Epilepsy is a cerebral disorder which develops suddenly, ceases spontaneously and has a tendency to recur. Usually it needs controlling by drugs. Haskell and Barrett (1993) report that it is a condition which affects up to 18.6 of every 1,000 people. There are a number of factors which can cause a fit. These include physical illness, emotional and physical strain and the inadequate administration of drugs to control the condition. However, those with this condition can generally successfully attend school without too many difficulties. Often, however, their condition will lead to under-performance.

There are a variety of types of epilepsy. Tonic clonic seizures (Grand Mal) is the most dramatic, where a child can have a fit, lose consciousness, have body spasms and sometimes loose control of their bowel or bladder. A facial fit will manifest itself in a similar way, except that it may not affect the whole body. Absence seizures (Petit Mal) often appear as a momentary lapse of attention. As a consequence of petit mal, concentration will have been lost and instructions will have to be repeated. Myclonic epilepsy is indicated through brief muscle contractions or distentions in the neck, while akinetic epilepsy is a situation where a child may drop to the floor momentarily and recover. In some circumstances the different types of seizures can combine in one person.

In many cases the lifestyle of the epileptic is no different from that of anyone else. The British Epileptic Association suggests that as few restrictions as possible should be placed on the child. It states that on some occasions rope-climbing activities may be unwise but providing there is supervision there is no need for other restrictions. Swimming usually causes no problems and this should be encouraged with the provision of a lifeguard at the side of the pool.

It is useful to know what actions to take in the event of an attack. The best approach is to:

- keep calm yourself and reassure the other children in the room;
- loosen the child's clothing in the neck region;
- place the child in the recovery position, with the head on its side;
- never put anything in the child's mouth;
- monitor the child's eyes and facial colour;
- check the breathing and the pulse rate;
- monitor the length of the attack: if it lasts more than five minutes call a doctor.

Muscular dystrophy

Muscular dystrophy is a wasting disease which has no known cure. It is a condition which does not affect the brain but does affect motor skills and therefore levels of personal independence. There are various types of the disease, with differing severity, the most severe being the Duchenne type which typically leads to death during the teenage years.

As the influence of the condition increases it is often necessary to make decisions affecting the location of the child's educational provision. For some children there will be increasing difficulties as the effects increase and there may be need of a home tutor; others will need a placement in a special school.

The child, their family and friends, and the teacher, all need to be knowledgeable about the disease and prepared for the eventual consequences. In the mainstream school, death is rare, since children with severe forms of the condition will have left before this is likely. However, a mechanism will need to be in place to meet such an eventuality.

Spina bifida and Hydrocephalus

Spina bifida and Hydrocephalus are typically related conditions resulting from a lesion in the spinal cord which is discovered and operated on shortly after birth. For some children the condition is mild and has little effect on their lives; for others, however, its manifestations are much more serious, leading to severe physical disability and possible learning difficulties. Hydrocephalus is caused by an increase in the pressure of fluid around the brain, often as a result of spina bifida. If it is left untreated it can lead to brain damage. A shunt is usually implanted at the side of the child's head in order to allow fluid to drain into the body. These shunts do get blocked from time to time resulting in children becoming sluggish and losing concentration. When this occurs they need to be hospitalised for the shunt to be unblocked.

Children with spina bifida often have problems with mobility and incontinence. Walking aids and wheelchairs are often required, as are various devices to deal with the incontinence. These problems can also be accompanied by difficulties with:

- judging size, distance or direction;
- forming concepts;
- fine motor control;
- personal organisation;
- emotional and social difficulties;
- moderate, severe or specific learning difficulties.

It is therefore essential that an individual assessment is undertaken so that good planning can be undertaken to meet the specific needs of the child.

Summary of strategies for mainstream class teachers

Strategies that may have to be adopted are:

- find out exactly what the child's difficulties and needs are, from parents, previous teachers and specialists;
- have contingency plans in place for emergencies;
- ensure that the child has all the physical aids they need;
- ensure physical access, e.g. ramps into buildings, handles in toilets;
- make sure the child is able to sit comfortably, in a good position to see;
- adapt activities so that the child can participate in physical education;
- provide maximum access to information and communication technology;
- allow more time for the child to complete tasks, and rest periods to prevent fatigue;
- arrange for other children to act as buddies/helpers;
- be understanding about time off needed for therapy or hospitalisation;
- send homework when the child is off school;
- do not lower expectations or pamper the child because of the disability.

Communication difficulties

Speech and language difficulties often co-exist with other disabilities, especially hearing impairment, cerebral palsy and moderate to profound levels of learning difficulties. Thus, the majority of children with more severe degrees of speech and language difficulties are found in special schools or units in mainstream schools. However, mild to moderate levels of such difficulties are common in mainstream classes. Language and speech are both vital components in the learning process and for those with difficulties in this area there will be consequent problems. Therefore it is important for teachers to be able to identify children with communication difficulties and ensure they get help.

There are four types of communication difficulties found in mainstream schools:

- articulation problems (e.g. substituting r for w in speech);
- fluency problems (e.g. stutter);
- voice disorders (e.g. hoarseness or high pitched voice);
- delayed or disordered receptive or expressive language.

Webster and McConnell (1987) and Martin and Miller (1996) have categorised several types of language delays: global, developmental, language disorders, environmental difficulties and social class difficulties.

Global delay

Global language delay exists when the general level of ability of the child, and not just their language skills, lag behind that expected for their age group. An example of global language delay is a child with Down's syndrome.

Developmental delay

Developmental language delay is related to the area of language and speech development only. Other aspects of development are not of concern. An example of this is a child suffering from auditory perceptual difficulties, whose language skills are delayed but who otherwise is developing normally.

Language disorders

Language disorders generally involve delays in both language development and in the language patterns exhibited by the child. Children in this category typically experience considerable difficulties and will need help from speech therapists. Most common among these children are those who are referrred to as aphasic or dyspraxic, which have been discussed earlier. Aphasic children have problems in understanding spoken language and are unable to use it appropriately. Dyspraxic children are unable to programme their speech muscles to produce sounds for acceptable speech. These disorders result in children experiencing considerable difficulties in learning generally, and in developing literacy skills in particular.

Extra help needs to be provided in the most difficult cases by specialist teachers and therapists, who may work on a one-to-one basis with the child. Those with less severe problems in the mainstream school will exhibit difficulties in communication. In question and answer situations during lessons they are unlikely to join in, even when asked directly by the teacher, and may be reluctant to do so even in small group or one-to-one situations.

Environmental difficulties

Environmental language difficulties are manifested in the living conditions of children. In some cases where parental language is limited, the children will have similar difficulties. This can also be the case for children where both parents are deaf or where the first language of the home is not English.

Social class difficulties

Conditions relating to social class have also been identified as being related to language development. However, this area is contentious. Bernstein (1970) and Tough (1977) argued that at the preschool stage pupils from disadvantaged homes were much less likely than middle class children to use language in complex ways. From this assertion the view emerged that there was a gap between children from different social classes in respect of their language development. It has also been argued that cultural differences, particularly in the early years of development, have a marked effect on the performance of a child in school. Factors such as the interaction between mother and child, the language patterns at home, attendance at nursery school and the attitude of the parents to school could, it was suggested, have considerable effects on a child's language development.

More recent research however, indicates that this situation is not so clear-cut. Tizard and Hughes (1984) argued that there is considerable overlap between social classes in language development. Nevertheless, because language acquisition is so important in children's achievement at school, particularly in the development of literacy, language enrichment programmes may be necessary to aid the development of some pupils.

Facilitating language development

Miller (1996) indicated that many language difficulties will be resolved naturally through the variety of activities provided at home and school. In this respect she advises a policy of professionals working together with parents. Where problems remain, Webster and McConnell (1987) argue for a 'naturalistic' approach through the spontaneity of the use of language.

As part of this, they advocate an integrated approach with a flexible support system to maintain it. Furthermore, they emphasise the importance of classroom management techniques such as gaining the attention of the child, having a sense of purpose, regular and systematic feedback, focusing on and isolating the main features of the tasks, checking instructions and providing positive feedback to the child. These are discussed in greater detail in Chapter 8 which deals with classroom management issues.

Summary of strategies for mainstream class teachers

Strategies that can be adopted to help children with communication difficulties include:

- listen to children carefully to determine speech/language difficulties;
- be a good model of appropriate speech and language;
- seat the child with others who are good speech models;
- use rhymes, etc., to encourage clear articulation;
- use role-playing, debates, puppets, etc., to develop oral language skills;
- use audio/visual aids such as video/audio recorder or language master;
- use language children can understand; simplify complex statements;
- use non-verbal clues, e.g. gestures, body language, visual aids;
- define, highlight and reinforce new vocabulary used;

- use cooperative learning to encourage discussion;
- be patient with stutterers; give them time to express themselves;
- accept the verbal contributions of all students;
- refer on those with complex problems to a speech/language therapist;
- use self-esteem/confidence building exercises;
- work closely with parents.

Further reading

Batshaw, M. L. and Perret, Y. M. (1992) *Children with Disabilities: A Medical Primer* (3rd edn). Baltimore: Paul H Brookes.

Cumine, V., Leach, J. and Stevenson, G. (2000) *Asperger's Syndrome: A Practical Guide for Teachers.* London: David Fulton Publishers.

Gilbert, P. (1996) *The A–Z Reference Book of Syndromes and Inherited Disorders* (2nd edn). London: Chapman and Hall.

Kersner, M. and Wright, J. A. (1996) *How to Manage Communication Problems in Young Children.* London: David Fulton Publishers.

Martin, D. and Miller, C. (1996) *Speech and Language Difficulties in the Classroom.* London: David Fulton Publishers.

Worthington, A. (ed.) (1999) *The Fulton Special Education Digest: Selected Resources for Teachers, Parents and Carers.* London: David Fulton Publishers.

CHAPTER 5

Children with emotional and behavioural difficulties

Introduction

The Code of Practice (DfE 1994a) noted the need for schools to take into account those children who display emotional or behavioural difficulties. The Code therefore includes this group of children who previously had not been placed under the special needs umbrella.

Children described as having behavioural difficulties or emotional and behavioural difficulties (EBD), although often clearly identifiable to the classroom teacher through their attitudes and activities, do not form a homogeneous group for whom help is easily provided. Rather, children with EBD comprise a group which is loosely formed, often by subjective means and decisions that are based on the quality of individual relationships between teachers and pupils.

This chapter focuses on the causes, identification and characteristics of children with EBD, the psychological models that are available to help with their management, and a summary of the most useful strategies to help alleviate their difficulties.

Causes of EBD

An analysis of the causes of EBD shows that these can be linked to both psychological and social factors. Visser (1999) identified four main factors: organic disorders, psychological problems, mental health problems and delinquency. The best known example of an EBD considered to have an organic causation is ADHD, which was discussed in Chapter 4.

Rutter and Smith (1995) have discussed psychological and mental health problems relating to EBD at some length. This includes clinical depression, anorexia nervosa and bulimia, as well as teenage suicides. Both Rutter and Smith (1995) and Pedlow (1999) have argued that the incidence of such disorders among children and young people have increased during the last few years.

Law and Rimmer point out that mental health problems affect at least ten per cent of children, particularly those in late adolescence. This is because some illnesses, such as schizophrenia, clinical depression and manic depressive disorders, do not manifest themselves until the late teenage years.

The last causal factor identified by Law and Rimmer is delinquency. Cole, Visser and Upton (1998) argue that schools for children with emotional difficulties straddle the divide between EBD and delinquency. In their view delinquency is a subjective label attached to children, which is largely dependent on the views and the terminology of the agency dealing with them.

Identifying pupils

The term 'children with EBD' is imprecise. The Code of Practice indicates that children with EBD can be placed within the wider group of children having SEN without providing any clearer definition of who they are. The Code suggests that children with EBD appear on a behavioural continuum between those who display challenging behaviour that is within normal limits and those who display indications of serious mental illness.

As a consequence of this continuum of severity of EBD, a continuum of provision has also been identified (Topping 1983, Upton 1983, Visser and Rayner 1999). This provision stretches from arrangements that are made for a small group of individuals in mainstream schools to separate provision in special schools or secure units.

It is not only the definition of EBD that causes problems. The number of children with EBD is difficult to ascertain. Historically, calculations have been based on the number of children who, as a result of their difficulties, were not in attendance in mainstream schools or had been excluded from school altogether. Laslett (1977) reported official statistics indicating that up to 10,000 children were receiving special help for emotional or behavioural difficulties, while Visser and Cole (1996) estimated some ten years later there were some 15,000 children attending EBD schools, as well as others attending pupil referral units (PRUs) and in hospital provision. In addition to this, recent DfEE statistics showed that some 12,000 pupils had been excluded from mainstream schools in England and Wales (DfEE 1997b).

Characteristics of children with EBD

The characteristics of children with EBD can vary widely. Ullman and Krasner (1965) and Leech and Raybould (1977) indicate that the manifestation of EBD is often dependent on the individual child and the particular environment. Smith and Laslett (1993) argue that the description is given to children who have great difficulty in making and sustaining relationships with others. Williams (1999), in a survey of staff in schools in Birmingham, found that the most common adjectives used to describe children with EBD were 'disruptive' and 'aggressive'. Smith and Laslett (1993, p. 58) go further, using adjectives such as selfish, inconsiderate, unacceptable, unapproachable, remote, demanding and impetuous, adding that these are emotions other pupils find unpleasant or frightening.

Smith and Laslett (1993), along with Greenhalgh (1994), while arguing that behaviour does not always originate from within the child, also point out that behaviour can have causal factors outside the control of teachers. Evidence from a survey for a London Weekend Television (LWT) programme (reported by Kelner (1993)) found that many parents lacked confidence when managing and disciplining their children. This survey also found that over a quarter of parents questioned felt that their children were out of control, while one third found disciplining them a problem.

Some children have experiences within the family, leading them to believe they are unwanted or unloved. In such circumstances children may be led to feeling they are unworthy, undeserving or unsuccessful. This can also lead to a lack of self-esteem, feelings of failure, alienation or insecurity. In such circumstances their teachers have great difficulties in establishing positive relationships with these pupils. Smith and Laslett (1993) point out that these children have a very limited repertoire of responses to situations and matching their behaviour to the expectations of others.

Greenhalgh (1994) argued that a child's behaviour is based on simple personal constructs, linked to individual value judgements of what is acceptable or unacceptable in different social situations. What may be acceptable behaviour within the family may not match that expected when visiting friends or within the school classroom. Children need to acquire these skills at an early age.

Research has consistently shown that children with EBD have learning difficulties. Rutter *et al.* (1970, 1979) found that there was a link between pupils with severe reading difficulties and poor classroom behaviour. Wilson and Evans (1980) showed there was a link between poor behaviour and educational attainment and Galloway *et al.* (1982) found that children with behavioural problems often had SEN, particularly learning difficulties.

Management

A number of psychological models are available to guide practice in working with children with problem behaviour. The four most widely used models for intervention are: the behaviourist approach, the cognitive or cognitive-behavioural perspective, the ecosystemic perspective and the psychodynamic approach (Ayers *et al.* 1995). Of these models, Ayers *et al.* explained that the first three may be helpful for working with children with behavioural problems in the classroom. These are discussed below.

The behaviourist perspective

The behaviourist perspective is based on learning theory. It is based on the principle that behavioural and emotional problems occur through inappropriate learning, and that a child with problems can be assisted through the acquisition of appropriate responses and through relearning techniques. The approach is subdivided into two theories: classical conditioning theory, and operant conditioning theory. Classical conditioning is based on conditioned associations between stimulus and response demonstrated through the work, largely with animals, of early pioneers such as Pavlov. Operant conditioning occurs when a person's behaviour is modified through a programme of reinforcement of positive behaviours. In such an approach a child will learn acceptable behaviour through the use of rewards, their pattern and timing. Effective techniques include time out, response costs, contracts, progress charts and token economies. This approach is sometimes called behaviour modification.

The main tool of the behavioural perspective in the classroom is functional analysis of observable behaviour. Observations should be set around four features: the frequency of the inappropriate behaviour, the intervals between behaviours, its duration, and its latency (the length of time before a pupil performs a particular behaviour).

The behavioural perspective calls for specificity and should lead to a testable hypothesis towards changing the child's behaviour. Testing this hypothesis should lead to the use of both short and long-term goals, where rewards are available to the children. The goals should be based on SMART targets (specific, measurable, achievable, relevant and time limited).

The cognitive perspective

The cognitive perspective of behaviour management is based on three key principles: that changes in behaviour can be initiated, these changes can be monitored, and changes in behaviour are related to changes in cognition. This perspective calls for an assessment of a child's learning processes and how they affect behaviour. Through undertaking such an assessment and an analysis of what has been observed, changes in behaviour can be brought about. Assessments can be undertaken using a variety of techniques including self-report, observation, interview, and the use of published behaviour rating scales.

Self-report aims to assess a pupil's expectation, attribution and self-concept. This technique focuses on the circumstances in which the behaviour occurs and the pupil's reactions in specific circumstances. The approach also asks children to focus on their feelings about themselves and to explain behaviour that occurred in particular circumstances.

Direct observation of pupils can be a useful technique, particularly if fixed interval sampling or frequency recording techniques are used. The ABC approach described by Ellis (1962) is another helpful cognitive perspective approach. Ellis argues that behaviour can be analysed through a three-stage process based on the precursors to the event (what Activated the events), the thinking process of the child that initiated the behaviour (Beliefs), and the nature of the problem behaviour (the Consequences of the precursors and the thinking stages). It has been claimed that the use of such an approach allows the teacher to observe problem behaviour in a way that enables them to identify and clarify problems, look at alternative coping strategies, detail the steps needed to bring about change and offer help to pupils to change their behaviour (Rogers 1994).

A positive behavioural change can be measured in relation to developments in the pupil's belief that they have the power to effect and change their behaviour through their own efforts and where they no longer blame others for getting into trouble. Ayres *et al.*

(1995) argue that for this approach to work effectively, teachers need to ensure certain conditions are in place. In their view teachers must be realistic in their expectations, convincing when discussing approaches with their pupils, convey trust in them and have sufficient status in their pupils' eyes to influence their thinking.

The ecosystemic perspective

The ecosystemic perspective of behaviour management focuses on the way that children perceive their world and their understanding of the total interactions in which they are involved. In this perspective, emphasis is placed on understanding the context in which social interactions are conducted and the resultant behaviour. In any analysis based on this perspective, the teacher will need an understanding of the whole social and emotional environment of the child and take into account influences that are present not only within the classroom but also in the rest of the environs of the school, as well as outside school in the family home and its neighbourhood. This perspective includes the principle that children's behaviour is influenced not only by their own thoughts but also the thoughts and actions of those around them who are in a position to influence them.

In any such analysis the ABC approach described by Ellis (1962) may be of value, as may the use of sociometric techniques to ascertain a pupil's acceptance by their peers as well as providing information about their relationships and its structure within the teaching group.

Working with children with EBD

Analyses of strategies used with children with EBD indicate that there is a hierarchy that is based largely around the level of difficulty displayed by the child and the procedures employed within individual schools. There are strategies used by individual teachers and those used in conjunction with the pastoral system across the whole school.

On an individual basis commonly suggested strategies include the use of the following:

- praise where there is a positive response from the pupil;
- positive reinforcement using food, drink, desired activities, and privileges;
- contracts between individual pupils, or class groups, and their teachers;
- sanctions such as stopping a pleasant activity, and time out.

Smith and Laslett (1993) identified different types of pupils with EBD, with some of their classroom characteristics as well as some of the most useful strategies for working positively with them. They categorised four different types of pupil: the class joker, the disruptive pupil, the unpopular pupil and the saboteur. They suggest that the class joker fulfils a role within the whole class. In such circumstances it is important not only that the teacher works with the individual child but also analyses the dynamics within the classroom and considers their relationship with the whole class.

The disruptive pupil can emerge in a classroom where the prevailing mood of the whole class is negative. In such situations a leader can emerge to express this satisfaction. In these situations teachers need to address not only the behaviour of this individual but, more importantly, work on their relationship with the whole class and analyse what it is they are doing that causes the class to behave as they do.

The unpopular pupil who is victimised in the class by his or her peers needs helping individually. It is often the case that they are making unreasonable demands on their friendships with others, interfering with them, giving unsolicited advice or behaving in a way that is regarded as socially unacceptable by their peers. In such situations work is needed with individual pupils to point out that such activities are unacceptable and that they need to change their behaviour. It is likely that children will deny responsibility for what is happening or that it is their responsibility to do anything about it. Nevertheless, it is important that the child is made aware that they have a responsibility to others and that it may be their behaviour that is bringing trouble on their own head.

Some children with disabilities can be teased or shunned by their peers. This is not the same as the situation described above and here a whole-class approach is necessary in order to help the situation.

The saboteur is the child who enjoys the thrill of disrupting the class and baiting the teacher or their peers. Children like this have strategies for disrupting lessons through egging on others and setting up confrontations as a result of devious activities that are sometimes hard to spot in the classroom or are initiated in the playground or corridor where supervision is so much more difficult. In these circumstances teachers can have difficulty 'keeping their cool'. It is important to remain calm and not get involved in any confrontation or word play with the child. In such situations questioning the child at length and making assertions are best avoided. Explain what you have observed or heard, keep the initiative and deal with the situation. Other pupils will be reassured if you can deal with such situations as it can alleviate behaviour that they also dislike.

Many children with EBD call for a whole-school response since, in recent years, more children with such difficulties are identified in mainstream schools. An increasing number of schools have adopted whole-school arrangements. These have included the use of behaviour monitoring books, behavioural charts, behavioural contracts and self-monitoring sheets for use with pupils. Individual schools have generally adopted their own schemes to suit their own purposes and it is important that a new member of staff investigates the arrangements adopted in the particular school where they are working. A conversation with a member of the pastoral staff or the deputy head teacher can be very useful here.

The circulars (DfE 1994b) on Pupils with Problems, often called 'the six pack', strongly recommend that whole-school policies on behavioural management should incorporate:

- simplicity, straightforwardness, specificity: based on clear and defensible principles and values;
- positiveness, set in constructive terms clearly setting out what children can and cannot do;
- rules, which should be kept to a minimum and for which the reasons should be clear.

Rogers (1994) provided similar constructive advice for working with children with EBD. His advice includes:

- establishing mutually agreed rights, responsibilities and rules;

- minimising hostility and embarrassment;
- maximising the possibility of choice;
- developing and keeping the respect of pupils by self-discipline and control;
- following up incidents of poor behaviour and following through;
- delivering on promises you have made;
- encouraging your colleagues to support the development of pupils' self-esteem;
- seeking to reduce stress levels.

Gribble (1993) argued that such approaches help to maintain the dignity of the teacher and that by taking these approaches a mutual respect between pupils and teachers can be encouraged.

Useful strategies

Bearing in mind the evidence presented by Gribble (1993), Smith and Laslett (1993) and Rogers (1994) the following classroom strategies are useful when working with children with EBD within the mainstream school.

- Devising an individual behaviour management plan for children with behavioural difficulties.
- Rewarding appropriate behaviour consistently, using praise, stars, points, etc.
- Implementing effective punishments such as time out or the withdrawal of privileges.
- Providing a structured approach.
- Ensuring all students have work at a level at which they can gain success.
- Displaying rules for class behaviour generated by discussions with the pupils.
- Fostering a supportive classroom environment in which all are valued.
- Avoiding dealing with pupils in a confrontational manner.
- Seeing pupils after class to express dissatisfaction with their behaviour.
- Taking time to listen to pupils who may have problems at school or at home.
- Helping pupils to set targets to improve their behaviour.
- Liaising with parents to promote consistent management, e.g. home–school contracts.
- Working with colleagues to develop a whole-school behaviour policy.

Conclusions

Dealing with pupils with EBD is not easy. They exhibit a wide range of destructive anti-social behaviours, and strategies to deal with these are not easy to find. Such circumstances can be professionally taxing, and personally frustrating and stressful for the classroom teacher. Nevertheless, circular 8/94 (DfE 1994b) makes it clear that newly qualified teachers should be able to establish clear expectations of pupil behaviour and secure appropriate standards of discipline in order to create and maintain an orderly class-room environment.

It is also the case that children with behavioural difficulties, who are poorly managed in their early school years, have a greater chance of entering adult life badly educated, socially inept and lacking in confidence. Such children, the evidence suggests, often lose their will to learn and succeed.

Further reading

Cooper, P., Smith, C. J. and Upton, G. (1994) *Emotional and Behavioural Difficulties: Theory to Practice.* London: Routledge.

Cornwall, J. and Tod, J. (1998) *Emotional and Behavioural Difficulties.* London: David Fulton Publishers.

McNamara, S. and Moreton, G. (1995) *Changing Behaviour: Teaching Children with Emotional and Behavioural Difficulties in Primary and Secondary Classrooms.* London: David Fulton Publishers.

Smith, C. J. and Laslett, R. (1993*) Effective Classroom Management: A Teacher's Guide* (2nd edn). London: Routledge.

Visser, J. and Rayner, S. (1999) *Emotional and Behavioural Difficulties: A Reader.* Litchfield: QEd.

CHAPTER 6

Assessment of children with SEN

Introduction

Increasingly, the assessment of children is set within a framework determined by factors outside the immediate control of classroom teachers. What is taught and how it is assessed is heavily influenced by the requirements of external tests or examinations such as the Standard Assessment Tasks (SATs) and GCSE examinations.

However, it is important to realise that information about pupils' abilities and achievements can be gained from a number of important sources other than formal tests and examinations. These may include school transfer documents and reports, discussions with parents and previous teachers, teacher-made tests, analysis of children's work, observations of their behaviour and the results of screening tests given on entry to the school. A key issue when considering the assessment of children with SEN is the purpose of that assessment.

Purposes of assessment

There are several possible purposes for assessing children with SEN. These are outlined below (based on Macintosh and Hale 1976, and Taylor 1997).

Screening: an important use of assessment is to identify children who have an SEN of one type or another. For example, screening tests can be used to identify pupils who have visual difficulties or those whose literacy skills are significantly delayed.

Diagnosis: another use of assessment is to determine a diagnosis of the type and severity of the SEN. For example, a diagnostic assessment is often needed to determine whether a child has a specific learning difficulty (dyslexia) or a mild or moderate learning difficulty.

Programme planning: various means of assessment are used to help in planning suitable programmes for pupils with SEN. For example, checklists of skills or teacher-made tests can be used to decide where to start teaching with a particular child.

Placement: another use of assessment is to decide on the placement of pupils in suitable ability groups, sets, special units or special schools.

Grading: a common use of assessment is to determine pupils' current performance levels, typically in comparison to that of other pupils. This will provide an estimate of the level of a child's educational needs.

Evaluation: a key purpose of assessment is to evaluate the effectiveness of teaching programmes. For example, assessment results will inform the evaluator of whether IEP targets have been achieved.

Prediction: assessment results can be used to predict the likely potential or future performance of a pupil or group of pupils.

Guidance: various forms of assessment such as inventories and questionnaires can be used to provide guidance regarding career decisions.

Approaches to assessment

Assessment can be either informal or formal. The SATs, when undertaken by pupils at the ages of 7, 11 and 14, are an example of formal assessment. Besides the evaluation of overall pupil standards their purpose is also suggested to include helping teachers to identify where further diagnostic assessment may be necessary.

However, this type of assessment is often of limited value to the teacher since the time lapse between each test is considerable and the information received too gross to be helpful in planning programmes. Teachers need to know much more detail about the performance levels of pupils in their classes. There are two ways of approaching this: by the use of other formal assessments or alternatively by using informal means.

If, for example, it is considered that greater knowledge of the reading skills of pupils would be valuable, a formal diagnostic test may at some stage be appropriate. However, informal testing can also provide much valuable information.

Informal assessment

In order to develop the skills of pupils, teachers must initially be able to identify a starting point for pupils within their classes. The experienced teacher, working with a new group of pupils, will not only spend time getting to know them but also in investigating what they have learned already. In this way the teacher is beginning the process of assessing pupils' needs and identifying starting points for teaching. Examples of informal assessment strategies in reading and writing are presented below.

Reading

An example of an informal test might include checking on the reading skills of the class by asking them, in turn, to read material selected from the course of study. This will provide some information about the appropriateness of the level of material which has been selected and will also help to identify pupils with particular strengths or weaknesses.

However, for those children where there is hesitation or apparent difficulty this approach will not be sufficient in itself. It will not tell if a child's difficulties are related to a number of crucial factors. For example, whether these are due to anxieties about reading aloud in class, possible visual difficulties, or if pupils have reading difficulties which need further investigation.

Similar procedures are appropriate for informally assessing the level of skill of pupils in other subject areas. These vary from subject to subject across the curriculum, but most teachers are able to devise ways of doing this in their subject area in order to find a satisfactory starting point for teaching and preparing differentiated levels of learning material.

Writing

An informal assessment of writing skills can be obtained from exercises involving copying from the whiteboard or flipchart. The skills involved in copying a piece of written work from the board, although patently simple to the teacher, may not be so easy for some of the children.

A simple exercise involves writing down the date and title of a piece of work or copying down the classroom rules. A walk round the classroom to look at what has been produced can be very revealing and can provide a good initial indication of some of the difficulties certain pupils may have.

This quick overview will not only provide an indication of copying skills but also will provide the teacher with an impression of the writing and fine motor control skills of the pupils in their classes. For example, at the age of 11 a typical mixed ability class will contain children covering the whole range of ability in this area; from those whose writing and presentation is precise and stylish to those who are still having difficulty in forming some letters correctly.

A point must be made in relation to the evaluation of writing skills. It is easy to relate poor handwriting or spelling to low overall ability but this is often not the case as some of the brightest children can have poor handwriting or even spelling. However, where there is a combination of weak reading skills, poor spelling and immature handwriting these are indications that further formal diagnostic assessment is necessary. It is only when this is completed that any true indication of the level of ability of the child can be made. It is in these circumstances that further professional advice and experience is needed. For example, it can be very useful to discuss your views with the SENCO who may already have information on the child or be able to conduct further assessments and suggest appropriate teaching techniques.

Other informal assessments

Useful informal means of assessing children's strengths and weaknesses include perusal of school records and discussion with parents and previous teachers. Full advantage should be taken of these valuable sources of information, but too often this is not the case.

A much used form of informal assessment is teacher-made tests. These produce information on children's mastery of the material which has been taught which provides clues about their performance in the various subject areas.

An often under-used type of informal assessment is error analysis of work samples produced in routine class work. Error analysis can be used to good effect in several curriculum areas. For example, it can be used to identify computation errors from arithmetic exercises, or regular spelling errors from written pieces, or phonic confusions from errors made in reading a passage. Error analysis enables teachers to pinpoint the specific difficulties pupils are having and thereby helps them to design effective remedial programmes.

Another form of informal assessment which can be of great use to teachers is continuous observation of a child's behaviour. Having the opportunity to observe exactly what a pupil does during a certain lesson can be very illuminating, as can tracking the pupil's behaviour in different classes.

Formal assessment

For some children informal assessments will not provide enough information for the classroom teacher. In such circumstances more formal assessments may be valuable. A number of factors need to be taken into account by teachers when considering formal assessment of pupils with SEN. These include:

- the specific purpose of testing a child, or a group of children;
- the range of tests which are available for use in the school;
- the differences between tests of potential (ability) and performance (achievement);
- the uses of the three main types of formal assessments: norm-referenced, criterion-referenced and process measures.

Norm-referenced tests
The best known example of norm-referenced tests are tests of learning potential. The measurement of cognitive ability or intelligence (IQ) is a familiar example of this. These tests measure a child on a given scale against a set of standardised scores and produce an outcome, typically reported as a quotient, which relates the child's score to the norm. The tests are therefore referred to as norm-referenced tests.

Other examples of norm-referenced tests are reading, spelling or mathematics tests which report their results in terms of an equivalent age which can then be converted into a quotient by dividing it by the child's chronological age.

Norm-referenced tests are useful in establishing the extent to which children are functioning above or below the levels expected for their age. They are therefore useful in identifying areas of strength or weakness and providing information on the severity of special educational needs. However, the information they provide is often of limited value in helping classroom teachers plan programmes to address pupils' SEN.

Criterion-referenced tests
Much more useful in planning educational programmes such as IEPs is the type of assessment referred to as criterion-referenced testing. In this type of test the child's performance is measured against certain criteria or particular levels of skill on specified tasks in order to indicate a level of competence. For example, the checklist of skills which children are expected to have mastered by the end of the Reception year represent one form of criterion-referenced test. Another example is a reading test which measures how

many of the 100 most regularly occurring words children know. At the secondary level National Vocational Qualifications (NVQs) are good examples of criterion-referenced tests, as are the standards for achieving qualified teacher status used in initial teacher training.

An increasingly used form of criterion-referenced testing is *curriculum-based assessment* in which expected outcomes of the school curriculum are the criteria used for assessment purposes. For example, assessment of progress towards National Curriculum attainment targets.

Process measures

Within the past few years alternative forms of assessment have emerged which have focused more on the process of learning rather than the final outcome. These approaches have been more concerned with assessing growth than comparing pupils with norms or criteria. Three such approaches are: performance assessment, authentic assessment and portfolio assessment.

In *performance assessment* pupils are requested to carry out a specified task which requires them to demonstrate their use of the skills needed for its completion. For example, pupils might be given various practical tasks which require them to demonstrate planning, computational, problem-solving, team work and leadership skills.

Authentic assessment is performance assessment applied to real life tasks. It involves the assessment of pupils' skills in conducting tasks such as: investigating why the fish in the school pond have died; producing a class newspaper; or setting up a small business from the classroom.

Portfolio assessment has been used in schools for many years in subjects like art where a portfolio of pupil's work is selected for assessment. It is now considered that it has great potential for assessing the progress and achievement of pupils with SEN, especially where the more formal measures used in schools (such as SATs) are not sensitive enough to assess the slower progress made by pupils with learning difficulties.

Portfolios are generally made up of work produced throughout the term or school year which has been selected jointly by teacher and pupil. Observable evidence of the pupil's achievements and progress is therefore available which is very useful for IEP meetings, annual reviews of Statements and parent–teacher meetings to review children's progress.

Formal assessment format

There are two formats used for formally assessing children in school. These are the use of group tests and individual tests. In both cases there is a wide range of material available. Individual tests are generally used by SENCOs or outside specialists such as educational psychologists who have the time and expertise to administer them according to the standardised instructions, whereas most group tests are suitable for administration by classroom teachers with minimal additional training.

It is advisable to discuss the use of formal tests with the school's SENCO who should be able to provide guidance on tests which are suitable for the assessment purpose which teachers have in mind. The advice of other teachers who have used such tests will also be invaluable.

Group tests

Group tests are tests which can be used with a whole class of pupils at one time. All have standardised instructions for administration and scoring which need to be carefully followed. Many are designed to be administered in a set period of time. These tests are usually relatively easy to mark. They can provide a quick method of assessing pupils' performance levels in basic skill areas such as reading, spelling and arithmetic. There are also group tests which aim to measure cognitive ability or learning potential but these require more expertise for their administration and in order to interpret the results.

Group tests are very useful for assessing the range and overall performance level of class groups and for identifying pupils whose poor scores suggest that further testing is necessary. However, scores from group tests must be interpreted cautiously as, for various reasons, they are not as accurate or reliable as scores from tests which are administered individually.

Individual tests

Individual tests are tests which can only be given to one pupil at a time. They are therefore more time consuming to use and also require more expertise to administer and to analyse the results. In most cases they are best given by SENCOs or specialists such as educational psychologists or speech therapists who have been trained to administer and interpret them.

Typically, following their informal assessment, possibly including the results of group tests, teachers will express concern about a particular pupil to the school's SENCO. The SENCO may then decide to conduct an assessment. This is when individual tests will be used to determine whether the pupil has a special educational need. Further testing is then carried out by the SENCO or outside specialist, such as an educational psychologist, to determine the type and severity of the SEN. When several individual tests or a battery of tests are used they can provide a profile of the child's strengths and weaknesses.

There are numerous commercially published tests available to assess a wide range of aspects of children's functioning. These include tests of:

- academic achievement: reading accuracy and comprehension, spelling, handwriting, mathematics;
- cognitive ability, creativity, language development;
- visual acuity, hearing loss, fine and gross motor skills;
- visual perception, auditory perception, phonological awareness, eye–hand coordination;
- personality, self-esteem, anxiety;
- adaptive functioning, life skills, vocational skills;
- interests, aptitudes;
- ADHD, dyslexia.

The class teacher's role in individual assessment is generally to refer pupils they have concerns about, following their informal assessments, for further testing to be conducted individually by the school SENCO or outside specialists. Another important aspect of the class teacher's role is to make sure they understand the test results communicated to them either verbally or in reports so that these can inform their teaching.

Further reading

Sattler, J. (1992) *Assessment of Children.* San Diego, Calif.: Sattler.
Taylor, R. L. (1997) *Assessment of Exceptional Students* (4th edn). Boston: Allyn and Bacon.

CHAPTER 7

Curriculum planning

Introduction

This chapter links closely with the previous one on assessment. Using an appropriate test will allow the teacher to obtain a baseline of what the child knows. It is from this baseline that their programme of work should be devised. This chapter discusses some of the issues raised with regard to planning programmes of work for children with SEN. It takes into account both theoretical and practical issues. The theoretical perspectives will concentrate on approaches to teaching, taking into account our knowledge of learning theory, and this includes sections on the learning domains, the importance of differential learning, and the theory of the developmental stages of learning. These models will be set in the context of the practical requirements of the National Curriculum regarding children with SEN.

The starting point for a child's programme of work is particularly pertinent and different subjects of the curriculum often need different approaches. Maths, for example, needs a strongly sequential approach in that skills often have to be learned in a particular order. With more able children there is a greater ability to generalise and understand not only what they are taught but also its wider application. The child with learning difficulties may have difficulty with retaining the basic information let alone applying it. Here the learning processes involved need to be broken down into short sequential steps.

Experience indicates that this is not an easy process for either the pupil or the teacher. From the teacher's point of view it is not always easy to break down the steps involved into pieces that are manageable for the child. Furthermore, it can be difficult to set the teaching out in the correct order for the child to understand the processes. Understanding for the pupil is more than half of the battle, for once they have got the concept of what the process involves the rest is usually easier. However, a further difficulty is the amount of time that it can take and the frustration involved for pupils and their teachers.

Planning as part of the teaching process

The literature on classroom organisation and management emphasises the importance of planning not only in terms of the development of the skills of the teacher (Cohen and

Manion 1983, Kyriacou 1991, Mitchell and Koshy 1993) but also in relation to the assessment policy of the school (DES 1989, Solity and Raybould 1988 and Wolfendale 1993).

Certainly, for most teachers, this skill is developed individually and is unique to them and their experience and expectations. Nevertheless there are common factors involved and models of practice have been developed. A basic model has been described by Mitchell and Koshy (1993) involving a three-point focus, described by them as the planning–learning–assessing dynamic. The model is seen as cyclical and progressive with the pupil and the teacher in a partnership together, as outlined in Figure 7.1.

This model has a definite starting point with the assessment of the pupil coming first. As part of the assessment process the need for evaluation of both what the pupil has done and the effectiveness of the teacher must be taken into consideration. Both aspects are critical to the development of good practice.

However, other key questions for those teachers working with pupils with SEN need to be addressed. The approach outlined in Figure 7.1, although useful, provides only a skeleton framework. Solity and Raybould (1988) have attempted to fill in some of these gaps. In an approach which they described as 'assessment through teaching', a five-point approach is recommended. This is outlined in Figure 7.2.

The approach presented in Figure 7.2 is much more detailed and is appropriate for use with children with learning difficulties. It provides a good framework for making teaching decisions. The model is particularly appropriate when the assessment/teaching strategy is being undertaken as part of regular classroom provision, and is seen to be integral to the daily routine of the teacher.

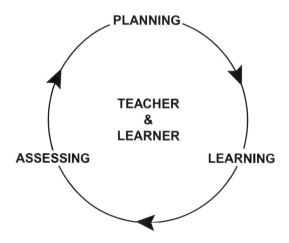

Figure 7.1   From the planning–learning–assessing dynamic described by Mitchell and Koshy (1993)

DETERMINING THE CURRICULUM SEQUENCE
What skills should I teach?
In what order should I teach them?

PLACEMENT ON THE CURRICULUM SEQUENCE
What does the child know now?

DECIDING WHAT TO TEACH
Selection and Sequencing

DECIDING ON TEACHING ARRANGEMENTS
Which methods should I use?

ASSESSING PUPIL PROGRESS
Evaluating the work done.
How to do this?
When?

Figure 7.2 The planning, learning and assessment cycle (based on Solity and Raybould 1988)

Assessing the progress of pupils

The question of when to assess the progress of pupils is also an important issue. In broad terms it must be left to the discretion of the individual teacher. In certain circumstances the assessment of progress may have to be done on a daily basis. In other circumstances it may be more appropriate for it to be undertaken at longer intervals. In normal circumstances in secondary schools this may be necessary because of the way in which the timetable has been organised whereby the teacher does not see the class every day.

Deciding priorities

In many respects the focus of the curriculum for pupils with SEN is determined by the requirements laid down in the National Curriculum documentation. However, for some pupils with SEN the selection of core material, the most fundamental of all knowledge for all pupils, can only deal with the basic requirements of coping and the foundations of independent living in the adult world.

In many respects the fundamentals of the academic curriculum content for children who have the more severe difficulties relate to the ability to read independently and knowledge of basic arithmetic. For some children at school leaving age these skills will still be a problem and they will have a continuing need for development. The figures nationally suggest that some 10 to 15 per cent of adults can be so defined, a figure which is not unexpected when taken in conjunction with the concept of the 20 per cent of pupils with SEN described in the Warnock Report and other similar documentation.

In both primary and secondary schools it is important that the learning diet for this group of children is wide and varied. As with any other pupils, those with learning difficulties need to be stimulated and set a wide variety of tasks to demonstrate their skills and build up their confidence. To concentrate merely on developing reading skills and on the basic four rules of number would be tedious for both the pupils concerned and their teachers. In a very short time such an approach would be self-defeating and of little value.

Working with the National Curriculum

The National Curriculum has, since the Dearing Review (Dearing 1993), set the teaching requirements in the main curriculum areas for most of the teaching week. The amount of time which can be spent on non National Curriculum activities varies at each Key Stage; for example Key Stages 1 to 3 allow 20 per cent of timetabled time to be used in this way. *A Curriculum for All* (DES 1989) set the requirements of the National Curriculum in the context of every child participating in a broad, balanced and relevant curriculum. Exceptions to this, the documentation implies, will be few, and often of a temporary or exceptional nature. Adaptations to the prescribed curriculum beyond this are minimal. The documentation stated that this should apply in three circumstances only, these being: for pupils with a particular kind of special need; for pupils whose special needs are likely only to be temporary; and individual pupils who are the subject of a Statement under the 1981 Education Act.

The subject orders describe the essential knowledge of each area of the curriculum. For many with special educational needs these are often too difficult and in this sense the teacher is left with the dilemma of deciding what should be regarded as the essential core knowledge for this group of pupils.

The flexibility of this arrangement comes with teachers' freedom to determine their own teaching approaches and the ways of delivering the programme. This is not just the case for those pupils with SEN but for the class as a whole. In reality this is a situation which has caused some difficulties and there is evidence to indicate that staff face the dilemma of attempting to accommodate the requirements of the National Curriculum with the level of work of some pupils with SEN in their classes.

For pupils with learning difficulties the problem of poor short-term memory is crucial. It is unrealistic to expect children with this problem to retain information even over a short period of time if no form of support work has been undertaken in the intervening period.

In some circumstances children will forget not only the task which was set but that it had been set in the first place! For these children, the reinforcement of work done, often through repetition and over-learning, is a key strategy.

Levels of work

An important part of the work of classroom teachers concerns making decisions regarding the development of learning for their pupils. These decisions are wide ranging, but among the most important are those relating to curriculum content and the level of under-standing, skill or experience which is regarded as acceptable from a particular child or group of children.

Teachers have to decide the level of work that is appropriate for the groups they teach. Sometimes this will be similar for each pupil. They must all finish their picture, copy down the work from the board, or they must all have reached the end of the questions for home-work. In other circumstances the level of acceptable work will vary, with the more able perhaps being expected to produce a certain amount of written work while only a few lines will be acceptable from those who are less capable.

In the first place, teachers have to decide what will be the core information that they consider a child should have and what is perhaps more peripheral. In the broad context this decision is implied very strongly through the requirements of the National Curriculum framework. Although of considerable value in an overall sense for most pupils, for pupils with SEN this approach is not really adequate. For the child with learning diffi-culties who is finding their classroom work difficult, the pace of learning expected can be a problem, as may be the depth of understanding which is demanded.

A child's level of intellectual functioning will vary according to their ability and their interest in the subject. For those children with SEN, the depth of information they can deal with can vary considerably according to their difficulties and their interest in the subject. Matching these factors with the requirements of the National Curriculum can be a source of considerable frustration for both them and their teachers, particularly where there is a mismatch of expectations. A better understanding of the practicalities of this can be understood in relation to the work undertaken on the development of learning domains.

Learning domains

Our understanding of how children learn and their ability to access knowledge, skill and understanding is based on theoretical underpinning from educational theory through the study of human behaviour. Our understanding of how individuals learn is based on models demonstrating different levels of difficulty relating to personal knowledge and understanding. These models cover three main areas of learning, described as domains. These are called the *psychomotor*, the *cognitive* and the *affective* domains.

The *psychomotor domain* is concerned with physical skills that need practice, e.g. changing a car wheel. The *cognitive domain* relates to the acquisition of knowledge, such as the capital cities of different European countries or the dates of important battles. The *affective domain* is concerned with the acquisition of attitudes, feelings and emotions and the development of personal attitudes and behaviours, from, for example, behaviour that is copied from that of significant others, to that which is based on internalised values such as an understanding of the concept of equal opportunities or anti-discriminatory behaviour.

Dave (1975) produced a five-stage hierarchical model illustrating the different levels of learning and understanding within the *psychomotor domain*. This led from the initial stages of *imitation* (observing skills and repeating them) and *manipulation* (performing skills according to instruction, rather than observation) to *precision* (accurately performing a skill independently) to the higher order skill of *articulation* (putting together one or more skills consistently) and *naturalisation* (completing one or more skills easily to where it becomes automatic).

Bloom (1960) identified a six-stage hierarchy of levels within the *cognitive domain*. The initial stages were described as *knowledge* (referring to the recognition and recollection of information) and *comprehension* (the interpretation and summarisation of information). The third level Bloom described as *application* (where information is used in a situation that is different from the context in which it was originally learned). The higher levels were described as *analysis* (where a pupil can see the interrelationship between known information), *synthesis* (where information is used to form something that is new) and *evaluation* (where decisions are made based on a personal justification or rationale).

Krathwohl *et al.* (1964) described a five-stage model for the *affective domain*. This includes the initial *receiving* (passive stage) and *responding* (complying to social expectations) stages, the *valuing* stage (where behaviour is consistent with personal values) and latter stages, described as the *organising* (where a pupil is committed to a set of personal values) and *characterising* levels (where behaviour is consistent with internalised values).

Another area of concern is *differential learning*. This was described in some detail by Brennan (1985) who made some important points as far as those pupils with SEN were concerned. His model divided the areas of knowledge and skill into three separate aspects. These are shown in a simple form in Figure 7.3.

In this respect, teachers of pupils with learning difficulties in particular have to select, as part of the initial planning for lessons, which level to aim for. It has been pointed out in both official documentation and research papers that the choice of level made by

---

What a child COULD know

What a child SHOULD know

What a child MUST know

Figure 7.3   Differential learning priorities

teachers for this group of pupils is often too low for the children they are considering. Brennan (1985), and others, have been at pains to point out the need for teachers to raise their expectations of pupils and to provide them with material and ideas that are both stimulating and challenging for them.

The intention of the Dearing Report (1993) was to allow a more flexible approach to the content of the curriculum for pupils with SEN and perhaps, in turn, this will allow for a more realistic approach by the classroom teacher in meeting both the personal and educational needs of the children.

This model acts as a guide to the teacher in conjunction with the points made earlier in the National Curriculum documentation in each subject area. To a large extent the subject areas describe the core points for each area of the curriculum. However, experience indicates that for many teachers working with children with special educational needs there are conflicting issues. Work which for the average and above average pupils can be accepted and assimilated easily as part of their normal learning process can produce considerable difficulties for pupils with learning difficulties.

Some children have had particular difficulties meeting the demands set out in the National Curriculum. The Dearing Report attempted to address, at least in part, some of these difficulties. The report's intention was to allow a more flexible approach to curriculum content. It is hoped this will enable classroom teachers to take a more realistic approach when producing programmes to meet both the personal and educational needs of their pupils.

The recommendations of the Dearing Report and more recent Government-led initiatives (DfEE 1998d) has resulted in a greater flexibility in the National Curriculum, mainly at Key Stage 4. However, the increased flexibility has provided an opportunity for some older pupils to gain work-based learning or early experience in an FE environment. It has been suggested (DfEE 1998d) that such a programme may help disaffected pupils to gain a better understanding of the relevance of school to personal learning and their future work prospects.

The instructional hierarchy

The idea of a level of instruction is related to the level of difficulty of the task that is set for a child. This can best be explained by remembering that demand for recall of events is easier for a child than those posed in a problem-solving situation; just as asking them to describe an event presents an easier task for children than asking them to explain how or why it happened.

Haring and Eaton (1978) identified five levels of an instructional hierarchy. Strategically the teacher is at liberty to use one or all of these as part of their teaching. This hierarchy is described in simple terms in Figure 7.4.

It is within the context of this model that teachers have to select their strategy when determining the level of skill required of the pupils in their classes. Factors affecting this choice cannot be solely determined by the views of the teacher but must also bear in mind the level of ability and understanding of children.

The Instructional Hierarchy

ACQUISITION

Where pupils are shown something for the first time and learn how to do it accurately.

FLUENCY

When children practise the skill until it becomes second nature to them.

MAINTENANCE

When children can perform the skill even when no direct teaching is continuing.

GENERALISATION

When children can use the skill they have been taught in a different context.

ADAPTATION

A situation where children will be set a problem which demands application of the skill by them independently.

Figure 7.4   The instructional hierarchy (based on Haring and Eaton 1978)

Developmental stages of learning

It is vital to take into account the cognitive skills of individual children in the classroom and their ability to acquire, process, organise and retain information. Learning theory on factors that affect children's ability to learn has been particularly influenced by the work of development psychologists such as Piaget, Vygotsky and Bruner.

Piaget
Piaget, through his observations and discussions with children, described learning development in terms that were developmental and which could be linked, in general terms at least, to the mental age of the child. Several models have been developed to describe his ideas in simple terms. Perhaps the most popular and accessible is the four-stage process outlined in Figure 7.5.

As far as mainstream schools are concerned, most children will arrive at the *pre-operational* stage. This stage is divided into two distinct parts. The first of these Piaget described as the *pre-conceptual* stage, the second as the *intuitive* level. At this point children's thinking is based on impressions rather than reality. Piaget illustrated this point through the use of a number of experiments related to what he described as conservation. These indicated that children were at a stage where they could not reason reliably, and where sometimes their reasoning would bear little resemblance to reality.

It is at the *concrete operations* stage that a child's reasoning skills become more realistic. At this stage a child has learned to conserve information to the point where they are able to develop reasoning skills at a level where Child (1993, p. 147) puts it, 'the child's attention is no longer fixed in one dimension'. Piaget argued that at this level the child

Stage	Mental age (approximate)
Sensori-motor	0–2 years
Pre-operational	pre-conceptual (2–4 years) intuitive (4–7 years)
Concrete operations	7–12 years
Formal operations	12 years upwards

Figure 7.5 Piaget's stages of development

would learn sequentially and that for most children this would take the form of a set pattern. This is perhaps best illustrated through examples from maths, where he argues that children learn to conserve ideas about weight before volume since the ability to conserve numbers appears before that of area.

Piaget calculated that only some 15 to 20 per cent of the age group at their time of leaving formal schooling would have arrived at the highest level of thinking he had identified and which he described as the *formal operations* stage. This stage is a level of thinking that is regarded as being well beyond that of many pupils with SEN in the secondary school, and particularly those with learning difficulties. However, this should not be taken as a hard and fast rule for all pupils with SEN. There are pupils with sensory or physical disabilities who are able to operate at the same stage as the rest of their peer group regarding their level of thinking. This is an important point for the management of learning by teachers and should not be forgotten.

The developmental stages detailed above not only help to set the developmental framework for learning and teaching but also help to identify the sequence of skills to be taught. Most pupils in the primary school, and those in the first year of secondary school, will still be working at the concrete operations level of thinking. For those with learning difficulties, as well as a considerable percentage of their slightly more able peer group, this is a level of operation that will not change throughout their secondary schooling.

The most important implications of the views of Piaget for those with learning difficulties can best be summed up as follows.

- Parents and teachers should be sensitive to a child's developmental level and their ability to deal with information or the concepts that result from this. Asking children to deal with tasks that are too difficult for them will result in confusion and may cause them distress or frustration.
- In terms of teaching strategies and the ability to learn, the mental age of a child is more important than their chronological age.
- These children, even in the upper school in their GCSE years, need to begin their learning from concrete examples and any conceptual thinking that is required should be introduced slowly.

- Concept formation can only come through the use of the internalisation of the concrete examples used with pupils. For most pupils with learning difficulties this will be a long-term aim only and may not be achieved during their time at school. A teacher must not expect the impossible nor set their sights too high for children in these circumstances.
- Explanation should accompany experience. The teacher should explain exactly what is required and children need to be helped to understand not only what has been reached in the lesson but also how this was done.
- A careful record needs to be kept of the progress of children, so that developments that have been made are clear. This is important for both the pupil and the teacher.
- The use of verbal techniques by the teacher and the interaction between teachers and their pupils is a crucial source of learning for all children. This is accentuated in many pupils with SEN as speech is their main, if not only, source of communication. For some children their skill with spoken language compensates for weaknesses in other areas such as reading or writing.

Vygotsky

Vygotsky emphasised the importance of three elements in the process of learning. These were that children:

- respond to their environment through action;
- reflect on their own thinking through the use of language; and
- gain understanding in a variety of social settings through the influence of significant others such as parents, teachers, friends and peers.

Vygotsky argued that instruction is at the heart of human learning and that it is largely a cooperative activity between a more expert or experienced learner and one who is less experienced. He saw, as part of this process, that the more experienced learner would provide a learning framework or *scaffold* in the form of props and prompts, as well as encouragement, to the novice. In these circumstances children are able to accomplish tasks that they could not do on their own and their learning potential can be more fully realised.

It has been suggested there are a number of factors that can help effective learning as part of the scaffolding process. These include:

- *recruitment* – where the teacher secures the child's interest to motivate them towards the task;
- *reduction in the degrees of freedom* – where the teacher simplifies the task and breaks it down into achievable steps for the child;
- *direction maintenance* – where the teacher in the early stages of the task motivates the child to succeed; at later stages in the process the child should find the task motivating in its own right;
- *marking critical features* – where the teacher emphasises relevant aspects of the task to allow the child to judge their own success compared with the correct solution; and
- *demonstration* – where either the teacher demonstrates the correct solution or where an explanation is provided to a partially correct solution that has been presented.

Vygotsky claimed that there is a gap between that which a child can achieve on their own and the potential that might be achieved with more expert or experienced help. He described this gap as the 'zone of proximal development' (ZDP). Unlike Piaget, Vygotsky did not believe that children need to be 'ready' to learn something new. Rather, it was his view that significant others should provide children with activities set above their developmental level (but within their ZDP) to challenge but not demoralise them. As such, he offers a model of individual educability that is dependent on a child's aptitude as well as the size of their ZDP.

Vygotsky maintained learning and development is set in a social context. This social setting can occur in both formal and informal settings and places knowledge in a cultural framework that is embodied in actions and activities. In this context, he asserted, learning and development reflects children's cultural experiences, as well as their opportunities for learning.

Bruner
Bruner, influenced by the work of Vygotsky, extended thinking within the world of education. He offered an explanation of how children represent their world. He saw this as a three-stage process. The first (the baby stage) he called the *enactive mode*, is where thinking is based entirely on physical actions and uses neither imagery nor words.

The second stage (normally encompassing children from the age of three to six) he called the *iconic representation* stage. At this stage children represent their world through mental images. These images, Bruner argued, could be auditory, olfactory or tactile, and helped children to build up a picture of their environment although they may not be able to describe it in words.

Bruner described the third stage as the *symbolic representation* stage. At this stage a child is able to represent the environment. Initially this will be undertaken through the use of language, although later this may be done through other media such as number, music or art.

Bruner's three-stage model has superficial links to that produced by Piaget. However, there are major differences between them. In Bruner's view we do not pass through the stages in the way that Piaget suggests; rather, as our thinking develops, we use aspects of the different stages when the need arises.

Bruner, like Vygotsky, places great emphasis on personal experience. He stresses the importance of culture, family and education on cognitive development. He gave particular importance to the value of developing a child's thought processes through the use of more expert or experienced instruction.

Furthermore, Bruner places great emphasis in the development of language. In his model, children's thought at the iconic representation stage is dominated by their perceptions and their ability to restructure and reflect on these is limited. Bruner emphasises the importance of encouraging children to talk and write about their experiences in order to encourage symbolic rather than iconic representation.

Implications for teachers

Each pupil is unique and will develop learning strategies in different ways to others. An effective learning environment will help children to develop this in relation to their interests and capabilities. Without doubt, the more motivated a pupil is the more they will want to learn, and as a consequence the more they will learn.

There are a number of factors that need to be taken into account in deciding on the possible strategy to employ with pupils with special educational needs. These include:

- Pupils will learn more readily when they are actively engaged in structuring their own programme of work.
- Learning is best undertaken in a holistic way so that pupils will not feel restricted by the subject boundaries. Teachers should be willing to continuously adjust their expectations to meet this.
- Evidence indicates that those teachers and pupils who participate in risk-taking in the learning and decision-taking process are likely to enhance the pace of learning. It is important that pupils realise that making mistakes is an integral part of the learning process and that they should not be discouraged or put off by their mistakes.
- Social interaction fosters learning, therefore opportunities should be structured for various forms of social interaction in classroom activities. There are a number of ways of approaching this, with different sizes of groupings and different tasks for different activities. It is worth experimenting to see which works best with different teaching groups in different situations.

For children with SEN, the state of their mind-set and their feelings about learning are crucial to their success. These can vary not only from pupil to pupil but also with the same pupil from day to day, and teachers need to remain very much aware of this.

Target-setting

Setting realistic and achievable targets for children in their classes is a vital part of the teacher's role. It is a complex process, taking into account the ability of children, their pace of learning and prior knowledge. In this context accurate feedback on children's work is essential in order to set future targets as well as having an accurate picture of their current point of development.

The management of the curriculum offered to pupils with SEN, particularly those with learning difficulties, is vital. It is important that their work is accessible, well planned and prioritised appropriately so they can benefit from their entitlement to a broad, and balanced and relevant programme (Waugh *et al.* 2000).

The recent publication *Supporting the Target Setting Process* (DfEE 1998c) is useful for the classroom teacher considering target-setting for individual pupils in their class. This booklet sets out QCA/DfEE guidance on setting both academic and social targets for children with SEN. The targets set out a series of performance criteria based on work completed with teachers in some 500 schools. The guidance is described as being useful when working with children of all ages, and those with a range of SEN. It is not intended that the descriptors should replace individual assessment schemes presently used in schools; rather, they are intended to provide a framework by which the progress of pupils can be measured.

The curriculum

In many cases a child with SEN can cope adequately with the curricular programme of the mainstream school. Indeed many pupils with a Statement of special educational need have this as a requirement of provision. Male and Thompson (1985) argued that where this is the case a balance must be struck between the special needs of the child and the opportunity for them to participate in the widest possible general school curriculum. Male and Thompson also point out that ultimately this must take the form of a compromise based on the individual needs of children. In essence, it is more a question of pace and differentiation within the curriculum, as well as realistic expectations from the teacher.

Barthorpe and Visser (1991) argued for the principle of access and entitlement to the National Curriculum, and registered four important aspects of the curriculum for children with SEN. These were breadth, balance, relevance and differentiation. Curriculum breadth relates to the curriculum range that is available for children, the learning activities and range of attainment targets (ATs). Balance is concerned with the balance between timetabled subjects, between attainment targets and a child's pace for learning, as well as the interests of individual pupils and the requirements of the National Curriculum. Relevance is concerned with the suitability of the teaching resources available, taking into account the interests of pupils as well as differentiating to take into account their individual needs.

Differentiation

The skills used for differentiation relate closely to those involved in setting appropriate targets. Differentiation is concerned with correctly matching the work expected from pupils with their ability to do it. It is an important skill that needs to be developed by all successful teachers. Reynolds (1992) argued that differentiation skills need to be covered at initial teacher training level. Differentiation is a developmental skill that needs much practice to gain consistency. For those working with pupils with SEN, particularly learning difficulties, it is an area of particular importance.

Differentiation can be undertaken in a variety of ways. The skills fall into two major areas: the tasks set for pupils, and the assessment of the outcomes produced by the children. However, for those children with SEN, other factors are of importance. These may include: the child's level of ability; interests; previous experience in the area of learning; level of motivation; personal expectations; their learning style; the pace of their learning and completion of work; the expected level of performance relating to their ability; and the support provided to assist achievement by the pupil.

It is important to take the child's level of ability into account when considering the work they might complete and to set both realistic and attainable targets for them. Similarly, their personal interests and previous experiences need to be taken into account. Children generally learn best by being guided from the known to the unknown, therefore utilising their previous learning and experiences is vital. It is also important to take into account their preferred learning style and personal expectations of learning. Many children with SEN have to learn through the use of concrete examples or through handling physical objects. This should be taken into account when planning their learning.

Similarly, some children with SEN learn relatively slowly compared with some of their peers, while some lack confidence in their ability to learn. This needs to be recognised and taken into account. For example, reinforcement of learning through the repetition of activities may be an important learning strategy for some children with SEN. For others, a differentiation in language style and vocabulary might be necessary in order for them to gain access to the topic.

The nature of many special needs can affect children's ability to concentrate on their work to the same extent as the majority of their peers. Problems will occur with the pace of lessons because of factors such as the time allowed for the work to be completed as well as the difficulty of the tasks demanded of them. This can lead to fatigue and, in some situations, an inability to concentrate for more than a few minutes at a time. These difficulties may also lead to poor student motivation.

In some circumstances children with SEN may become tired more easily than other pupils, thus affecting their capacity for learning. Tiredness can most easily be observed in the afternoon and teachers should take this into account in their planning. If possible, new learning should be undertaken in the morning. The school timetable can render this difficult and in such circumstances a careful watch may need to be kept on vulnerable children. Tiredness is sometimes difficult to discern and close observation of a pupil's performance at different times of the day may be required. It is also generally the case that younger children are more prone to tiredness than older ones.

The importance of correctly addressing the level of ability of children with SEN is a major theme of this book and strategies covering aspects of this are important considerations throughout the book. For those looking to widen their knowledge on the wider issues of differentiation, Barthorpe and Visser (1991) is a useful starting point.

Homework

In theory there is no reason why pupils with SEN should not attempt homework in the same way as other members of the class. In practice some will be able to cope with the demands much better than others will. The success of this will depend largely on the individual nature of the problem and every case should be judged on its merits.

The question of the organisation and setting of homework is important for children with physical problems. Some children will need to leave lessons early to avoid congestion in the corridors. If work is to be set, it is important this is done before the end of the lesson, especially if children are to copy it down before they leave.

There is also the question of the physical fitness of children to do homework and the effect such an extra strain may have on their physical well-being. As with the points raised earlier about tiredness of pupils in class, individual teachers need to use discretion.

Further reading

Byers, R. and Rose, R. (1996) *Planning the Curriculum for Pupils with Special Educational Needs: A Practical Guide.* London: David Fulton Publishers.

Carpenter, B. (ed.) (1996) *Enabling Access: Effective Teaching and Learning for Pupils with Learning Difficulties.* London: David Fulton Publishers.

McNamara, S. and Moreton, G. (1997) *Understanding Differentiation: A Teacher's Guide.* London: David Fulton Publishers.

Waugh, D., Stakes, J. R. and Hornby, G. (2000) *Broad, Balanced and Relevant: Meeting the Needs of Children with Learning Difficulties Within the National Curriculum.* Hull: Halfacrown Academic.

CHAPTER 8

Classroom management

Introduction

This chapter focuses on the need for good classroom management strategies as an essential part of the role of the teacher. These, it can be argued, are a prerequisite for teachers in any situation, and for those working with children with SEN they cannot be emphasised too much.

There are various techniques available which the effective teacher can draw on and use as the situation demands. Knowledge in this area is acquired through experience and finding out what works best in which circumstances. It is not always easy to understand why one technique, although seemingly appropriate for two similar classes, is much more effective with one than the other.

Factors which may help explain this include the chemistry that exists between the members of the teaching group, the learning style of the pupils, and the relationship between the teacher and the pupils. For pupils with SEN, particularly those who have become disillusioned, or disaffected, an awareness of effective classroom management techniques is essential.

Teaching approaches

Cohen and Manion (1983) outlined six basic approaches to classroom management. These were:

- the *teacher-centred* lesson – in which pupils listen to the teacher and the session is conducted as a talk or a lecture;
- *active learning* – where there is discussion and mutual help between the pupils;
- the *lecture discussion* – where although there is a lecture format there is interaction between the teacher and the pupils;
- *independent planning* – where the pupils work in small groups and the teacher acts as an 'expert–consultant' among the members of the class;
- *group task-centred* – where the topic is the focus of attention and the group work in cooperation with each other as in a seminar situation;

- *independent working* – where the pupils work entirely on their own and there is little or no interaction between them.

Which approaches work best?

Children with SEN often have problems with concentration. The length of time they are able to concentrate on a task may be relatively short. In this situation it is important that teachers build a range of activities into their lessons. These can take into account not only the problem of the short concentration span but also allow for the development of the whole range of the senses in the programme of work. For some children this is essential to develop the more academic skills, as well as bringing variety and change to it.

What is certain is that some approaches with pupils with SEN will be more appropriate than others. Of those outlined above the least successful are the teacher-centred and the independent working approaches. Pupils with SEN work best and stay on task longer in a cooperative situation where they have an understanding of the classroom routine and a feeling of some control over the direction of their work.

Beyond this, the best approaches rely on a short, 'snappy' introduction to a lesson by the teacher and the pupils then being set tasks to complete. This approach is not without its problems. During the introduction the class will have to remain quiet, which is not always an easy task for either them or for the teacher. Furthermore, the amount of instructions the pupils can receive will have to be carefully thought out so as not to be so complicated it will confuse them.

The concentration span and short-term memories of some children can be surprisingly short. Some will find difficulties in listening beyond the first instruction given to them. With some classes, by the time the teacher has said 'come in, take off your coat, sit down' followed by 'take out your exercise book, find some thing to write with, open your book at the next page and write down the date', some pupils will still be looking for their book and will have not listened to any of the instructions which came after that! Careful observation of the class is essential in determining the pace at which the instructions should be given. In these circumstances, it is also important that the instructions are clearly understood and repeated if necessary for those who need.

Discussions

A further useful approach is to engage the class in a question and discussion session. However this approach can typically only be sustained for about ten minutes of a lesson. The advantages of this approach is that the pupils will have to do no writing, which is a bonus for many of the less able who find this task difficult. However, there are drawbacks to this technique. The first is that the pupils need the ability to listen to each other as well as to the teacher, something that can be sorely lacking in some classes. Some children will need training in this skill. To do this in a formal and organised way can be a difficult task. A great deal of teacher effort may be needed in setting this up if it is to be interesting and effective.

It is important to encourage participation from as many children as possible. One way of doing this is to work around partially correct answers that are given in the discussion and allow some discussion of what other pupils have said. These partially correct answers can be built up into complete ones. When setting up this situation it is important that the pupils feel comfortable with it, otherwise there is little chance of them contributing anything.

It is vital that the teacher is as flexible as possible in the way the situation develops, and allows discussions to incorporate things that the pupils feel are important to them and with which they feel comfortable. It should be remembered that in some cases far more will come from such a situation than could have been expected and those teachers who are prepared to take risks on deviating from their planned lessons can often benefit through the greater participation of pupils. It is important, however, to retain a sense of balance and to use discretion in such circumstances.

Written questions on the whiteboard/flipchart

A commonly used approach is to produce structured questions for a class either on work-sheets or on the whiteboard. This can be a useful way to allow the teacher to get round the class to help pupils individually. The best approach is to provide the easiest questions at the beginning. These should be written simply, in short sentences, and based on concrete examples, perhaps on work provided on the same sheet as the questions or on the whiteboard or flipchart which the children can do and which will give them confidence. The more open-ended conceptual questions are best left for the later stages of any work to be done. As suggested earlier it is unlikely that those pupils with learning difficulties will get to these. However, with a mixed ability class such an approach will be essential to deal with the needs of the most able. The issues raised here open up the whole question of the preparation and presentation of worksheets. This is a topic that is dealt with in much greater detail later in this chapter.

Reading aloud to a class

As mentioned earlier, pupils with learning difficulties work best when there is little writing to be done. Often other activities will appeal to them more as they will not be held back or feel inhibited by their weak writing skills. Many pupils at both primary and secondary level enjoy listening to a story read to them by their teacher, particularly if the teacher is able to read aloud well and is enthusiastic about doing so. Pupils with reading problems can get far more from a story this way than if they have to struggle through it trying to read it for themselves.

Using the teacher-led reading aloud technique has benefits in that pupils may decide to volunteer their services to read aloud. It is important not to discourage them to do so. A careful selection of the sentences, paragraph or few lines tailored for each child can be useful and lead to enhanced confidence in this skill.

Using the video

Gaining an insight into a story or play has been considerably enhanced by the video revolution. Most schools have video equipment and it is a useful tool in the teacher's armoury. The visual image can be of enormous benefit to children who are weak academically. It will not only help motivation but also enhance personal internalisation and encourage discussions.

Practical lessons outside the classroom

Be encouraged to go outside of the classroom to use the school and its environs for practical applications of what you have been trying to teach in the classroom. Properly organised, such experiences can be valuable and rewarding. Less experienced teachers are often wary of taking a class out of the classroom for fear of difficulties and pupils 'playing up'. The golden rule in this situation is never be conned into doing this by a difficult class looking for an easy lesson. It will not be so for the teacher! Only take them out on your own terms and make it dependent on exemplary behaviour leading up to the trip.

There are a number of activities that lend themselves very well to outdoor activities: survey work, interviews and mapping are some of these, along with a whole host of activities in maths. Work on the local environment of the school can be very useful in that the children will know where they are and be able to talk about it in some detail.

Using drama

Children who have difficulties with reading and writing often enjoy being allowed to act out situations in class. This can be a particularly profitable way of spending time if you are prepared for a certain amount of chaos in the build up and organisation of it. Pupils with SEN often prefer the extemporary approach to drama when they can put together their own scripts. Their difficulties with role-play can be quite marked. Often they find it very difficult to think themselves into the part and they find the empathy that is necessary for this particularly difficult.

Many pupils with reading difficulties prefer reading from a play rather than from a book. The continuous action in the play format appeals to them as does the short sharp sentence structure of the play as opposed to the more wordy descriptive approach of the novel or reader. They also like to take on the part of the character they are reading. This can be an enjoyable activity for all. Particularly popular are plays that they can see are humorous or relevant to their personal circumstances. There is an increasing amount of suitable material for all age groups available in schools.

Wall displays

Children of lesser academic ability can benefit greatly from putting together work for a wall display. Pupils with learning difficulties rarely have such opportunities as the work of others is often chosen as being better or neater. Therefore, having their work mounted on the wall can be a great boost to their confidence.

The cooperative nature of this work appeals to them as does the strong drawing orientation of the work. One very useful skill that can be introduced in this type of activity is that of tracing from books or other sources. Producing a wall display can often entail a research element and the use of library skills can be included in this activity.

Projects based on the study of local issues often make good topics for wall displays. Not only will this encourage the skills mentioned above but it will also allow the children to work on a topic which is familiar to them and which may encourage sensible discussion of topics of local interest such as bus routes, planning developments and the siting of local facilities.

The dangers of using the wall display technique are firstly that it can be overplayed to the extent that the novelty value wears off. Secondly, in the secondary school in particular, if teachers have a large number of classes it may be difficult to find space to mount all the displays in the classrooms where they teach. This can lead to disappointment and a certain degree of frustration in pupils.

Less successful activities

There are a number of approaches and teaching techniques that are generally not successful with pupils who are academically weak. These include:

Teacher talk. Most pupils in this category will not be able to follow a prolonged talk by a teacher unless the topic is of considerable interest to them and it is done at a pace and with language that is appropriate for their level of ability.

Listening to audiotapes. A similar point needs to be made about listening to audiotape recordings. With very few exceptions the concentration span for this activity is similar to that of listening to the teacher talk.

Dictation. In normal circumstances this is a total waste of time for most pupils in this category. They will not be able to take down notes that are read out by the teacher. They will not be able to spell the words required. Copying down at dictation speed is a nightmare for them and for teachers who will spend all their time repeating words or phrases that the children have missed. The approach is often a recipe for disaster.

Note-taking. A similar point needs to be made about taking notes from books. Even bright teenagers in their last years at school find it difficult to pick out the pertinent points from a textbook. For pupils with learning difficulties these difficulties become insuperable.

Unstructured written work. This too is a recipe for disaster, as children who have difficulty in writing things down will have difficulty also in coordinating their thoughts on paper. Children in this category will have difficulty in writing a paragraph let alone an essay!

Fieldwork notes. Writing up fieldwork notes is another task that can only be done within a structured framework devised and closely supervised by the teacher, otherwise chaos reigns and the level of frustration can be considerable for all concerned.

If some major piece of writing is required the Cloze procedure is the best approach, where some words are missed out. Even using this approach is not foolproof, and the missed out words may have to be written down for pupils to see. Even then the correct word for each blank may have to be pointed out to some individuals.

Recording pupil progress

The National Curriculum demands that a record of the work and progress of pupils is kept and varied formats for doing this have been developed in schools throughout the country. These have included written records, tick boxes, the use of charts by pupils or pie charts or graphs. However, records for those with SEN have been part of good classroom practice for many years. Many staff have developed a personal format for their own and the pupils' benefit. They then marry their records with the format demanded by the rest of the school to match the National Curriculum regulations.

A wide variety of possible approaches to this have been identified. This is because of the need to meet a large range of individual circumstances. However, analysis indicates that the formats used can be put into three distinct categories: those kept solely by the teacher, those where the pupils have a role in recording their own progress under teacher supervision, and those where progress is indicated through the use of checklists produced as part of a commercial publisher's scheme.

Records should be straightforward to keep and simple to access. Brennan (1985) indicated that essentially they should be individual, indicate progress and be signed and dated. He further suggested that the information detailed should show:

- the child's relevant problem areas;
- a record of attendance;
- progress – indications of when the work was started and when revision was undertaken;
- the dates when reviews were conducted and the results;
- a place to enter the results of standardised tests and SATs results.

The danger with record cards is their inaccessibility to vital information for all staff. In some schools, in order to avoid this problem the record cards of children with SEN are photocopied and distributed to all those who teach them. As part of the responsibilities of the SENCO (or the SEN department in larger schools) the learning, and therefore the teaching implications, are also detailed briefly. Despite this being an onerous task for those undertaking it, many staff find this a useful strategy. It provides them with valuable information and helps to focus their teaching strategies for these children.

Self-esteem

Meighan (1991) points out that research evidence shows that pupils tend to perform as well, or as badly, as their teachers expect. Views of children by significant others such as parents or teachers also influence a child's perceptions of themselves. Such a concept of self relates closely to personal self-esteem. This is the case for all pupils but particularly pertinent for those with general learning difficulties. It is the case that teachers' views and expectations of pupils are communicated to them frequently and often unintentionally, influencing the behaviour that follows.

Coopersmith (1968) showed marked variations in the behaviour of children with different levels of personal self-esteem. His study, which concentrated on boys only, categorised three levels of self-esteem. The results indicated that those with high self-esteem have a positive and realistic view of themselves and their abilities. Boys in this group were confident, not unduly worried by criticism and enjoyed participating in activities. These children, his study indicated, were generally successful both academically and socially. Those boys described by Coopersmith as having medium self-esteem had some of the qualities outlined above but were more conformist, less confident of their own work and more in need of social acceptance. Coopersmith described boys with low self-esteem as 'a sad group', who were self-conscious, isolated, reluctant to participate in activities, underrated themselves and were over-sensitive to criticism.

Self-fulfilling prophecies

Coopersmith's research supports the view that, in school, 'failure repels and success attracts'. In this respect constant failure or continually telling a child that they are a failure acts like water torture, producing a self-fulfilling prophecy through labelling. Rosenthal and Jacobson (1968) found that children fulfil the prophecies that others expect of them.

While criticisms of Rosenthal and Jacobson's methodology have been made, other studies have shown conclusively that positive attitudes and optimistic approaches do have a marked effect on the classroom performance of children. Nash (1972) for example, who compared the performance and behaviour of pupils with teachers' expectations of them, also concluded that the way pupils were perceived by their teachers had a great influence on their attainment. His study also indicated that teacher expectations of pupils had a greater influence on performance than any other factor. Sewell (1982) argued that teachers and parents act as an audience to the labelling of children. They are rarely passive or impartial and they play a part in the way a child learns about their identity.

Douglas *et al.* (1971), in a major survey, indicated that life chances were set around success or failure in school. As such it can be argued that these chances must be set in the context of personal self-esteem and the role of the teacher in developing this from an academic point of view at least. In this respect the labelling process within school must have a major impact.

In the context of developing children's self-esteem within school, it is important that teachers are aware of the work of Meighan (1991) who identified a four-stage process relating to labelling. These stages he described as:

- predictions about pupils that occurred before meeting them;
- experiences during the initial meeting;
- subsequent patterns of interaction between the teacher and the child;
- retrospective assessment and reflection by the teacher.

Discipline

It is an aspect of both primary and secondary schools that children who are less motivated and academically less capable are likely to provide the teacher with more challenging behaviour than some of their more able counterparts. This is more often emphasised when pupils with potential for poor behaviour are placed together for lessons when streaming or setting is used in a school.

Coping with unacceptable behaviour can provide real problems for the teacher, particularly the inexperienced members of staff or those who are new to the school. Without control of the class by the teacher then little or no teaching or learning can take place and chaos will result. Evidence from McManus (1989), Ayers *et al.* (1995) and McNamara and Moreton (1995) indicate that there are both avoidance strategies and modes of effective control which need to be considered by the teacher.

Avoidance skills

There are a number of pointers that should be born in mind that may be helpful if you find yourself working with a child with task-avoidance skills. These can only act as guidelines as both the situations and the personalities involved will be unique in each teaching situation. They include:

- Expect children to make mistakes and use a teaching model that will take this into account. Children need the freedom to make certain mistakes in an environment that allows them to correct their errors without fear of condemnation. Many pupils can see the effect of their mistakes and the social consequences of them for themselves and others around them. Explanation in such circumstances can be better than recrimination.
- Have a sliding scale of strategies for discipline. Some children will respond better to certain approaches than will others. Some will reach a level of understanding of the consequences of their behaviour before others, even though they may be the same age.
- Be decisive if a child openly defies you. If you allow them to get away with it, this will not only show them that they can but will give a lead to others of a similar attitude to try their luck. In situations where this happens it is often best to talk to the child away from the rest of the class so that you are not in danger of drawing

comment from them as well, which will only complicate matters often to your own detriment. It is often useful to make your comments in front of another, more experienced teacher as this lends weight to the situation.

Positive strategies

When there are problems on a regular basis in the classroom, positive discipline strategies work better than negative ones. It can be useful to have a set arrangement that is known by all the class. The use of a red card system to call for assistance from other staff is one commonly used example. If necessary adult help can be summoned by sending a child out of class to a delegated member of staff with the name of the offending pupil written on the card. An awareness of this routine can also help to dissuade others following the offender.

Do not get personally offended by the behaviour that is being shown. In many cases it is the authority which you represent rather than you as a person which they are attacking. All classes 'try out' a new teacher to see how far they can go and this is a common experience of teaching. To remain detached in this situation can be difficult, but to deal with a situation in a dispassionate way will be of much greater benefit in the long run. If a child, or even worse a group of children, can see that they can 'get you going' this will only give them encouragement for the future.

Get to know the names of the pupils as quickly as possible. A comment or question aimed at a particular child by name will be much more effective than a general point. In a situation where you are not sure about what is happening, a question to a pupil you think is involved will lead to a direct (if often negative response) from that person, as opposed to a question aimed in a general direction only. A general question will alert the offending group of your awareness and in some situations that will be enough, but often you will have to ask a follow up question, that should be aimed at an individual.

Separate immediately those who are causing you difficulty. You may have to physically reorganise the furniture in the room to do this. However, the effort is worth it. Classrooms in the secondary school can be set out in a variety of ways. The most formal is where they are in rows. From a discipline point of view this is the easiest way of keeping order since you can see every face. In some situations, where the classroom is not your own or it is a laboratory or practical area where moving the furniture is impossible, it is important that you have the faces of the chief troublemakers sitting towards you, often at the front of the room or even isolated (e.g. under the whiteboard) away from the rest of their friends.

Try not to get angry. If you shout, the class will often enjoy the situation even more. Use shouting and anger, acted or otherwise, for key situations. Then it can be really effective. To act out anger is a real and vital skill and very effective with a class, without your emotions being reduced to tatters.

Set standards and adhere to them. Set them in conjunction with the standards set throughout the school and the school rules. To allow a child to wear an outdoor coat in class, in other than abnormal circumstances, in a school where this is not acceptable can only produce difficulties for you. Similar points can be made about chewing gum, swearing, writing on the covers of textbooks, and even seemingly small points like standing up at the beginning or end of lessons.

Be consistent and persistent. If pupils' behaviour is reasonable and the general norm within the school, demand it from your classes. They will be expected to conform elsewhere in the school. Ensure you get the minimum standard at least. However, be realistic in your demands. You cannot expect to get the impossible. Older, long-term members of staff will guide you in this respect; ask them if you are not sure.

Avoid having victims and favourites. Do not let one child get away with something you have punished another for. This can only cause resentment and a sense of injustice.

Try to solve class discipline problems yourself in the first instance (although for a number of reasons there will be times when this is not possible and you will have to seek the help of others). Children will respect you more for dealing with the problems yourself. In the eyes of those not involved in the difficulty your ability to deal with the offenders is an additional plus. When a matter is something you regard as serious tell a more senior member of staff; the head of department or year head. Do not be afraid to do so, particularly if you have dealt with it. It is a good idea to tell the child that you will report a matter to another teacher. This not only indicates your thoughts on its seriousness but also keeps the pupil in the picture – a useful aid in helping to develop a positive relationship with them.

Discuss problem children with other staff. Their experiences with them may help to shed light on the pupil's difficulties and the conversation may also indicate that you are not the only one having trouble with a particular pupil.

Admit the problem exists. Without this being the very first step you can solve nothing.

Enjoy it! Be relaxed with your classes and they will also relax if you give them chance to do so. In general, pupils appreciate a gentler, good-humoured approach, rather than a hard and inflexible attitude. It is often easy to observe those who have the potential for trouble. In these cases concentrate on the positive and persuasive rather than the inflexible and Draconian.

Effective control

Evidence from McManus (1989), Cohen and Manion (1983) and Kyriacou (1991) confirms that effective classroom control is typically a difficult area for teachers. What teachers feel may be an effective deterrent to pupils is not always seen by them to be so. The evidence indicates that there are three key possibilities that are employed by teachers in school.

Verbal reprimands. Verbal reprimands can be effective if not used too frequently. Overuse can lead to the wishes of the teacher being at best ignored and at worst reinforce the undesirable behaviour. Where verbal reprimands are used they are best if brief, specific to the behaviour, stern, and coupled with indicating to the child the behaviour required. Quiet reprimands are far more effective than loud ones.

Detention and lines. Detentions and lines are used frequently by staff and although apparently successful with some children for many they are ineffective. Detentions are the more effective of the two, generally because they ensure the loss of valued free time. They are effective also because on some occasions, such as official detention, the child's parents have to be informed. Some parents will not allow children to be kept in after school hours. This can be an added difficulty and the way round it for the teacher is to keep the child in at break and lunch times for the required time. This is an added burden for the teacher but is often a necessary and useful deterrent.

Contacting parents. Wheldall (1991) indicated that children interviewed indicated that this was the most effective form of punishment. However, this can have problems for teachers who may be new to the school and have had little personal contact with any parent, where the parents are not supportive of the school or where the behaviour persists. In these cases a chat with the head of department or the year tutor can be very effective and may take the heat out of the situation. Contact with either of these people can also act as a deterrent to the future misbehaviour of the child.

Generally, disciplinary measures are more effective when they are:

- Immediate.
- Built upon a good relationship between pupil and the teacher.
- Consistent, systematic and predictable.
- Not positively reinforcing the undesired behaviour.
- Accompanied by clear indications of the desired behaviour.

Work by Wheldall and Merrett (1991) and McManus (1989) indicates that the best approach to class control is through a reward system that underscores good behaviour and work. This results in better behaviour and is seen as the correct approach by the vast majority of pupils. Children view a reward system that involves parents' knowledge of their progress as being the best approach. The evidence indicates that they prefer time when they have a choice of activities. In the primary school in particular, a choice of the lessons they preferred was seen by pupils as reward for good behaviour. Rewards are likely to be far more effective where they can be seen by their children to have been earned.

The development of classroom management skills is an important facet of working with children with SEN. Many of them find the process of schooling difficult. Those with learning difficulties in particular often see themselves as failures and become disenchanted and difficult. A positive attitude to their problems by their teachers is essential, as are knowledge and skills in developing suitable and appropriate programmes of work for them.

Further reading

Docking, J. (1996) *Managing Behaviour in the Primary School* (2nd edn). London: David Fulton Publishers.
McManus, M. (1989) *Troublesome Behaviour in the Classroom*. London: Routledge.
Smith, C. J. and Laslett, R. (1993) *Effective Classroom Management: A Teacher's Guide* (2nd edn). London: Routledge.

CHAPTER 9

Developing reading skills

Introduction

This chapter concentrates particularly on the development of reading skills for those pupils who have this difficulty. Firstly, some background information is provided on the National Literacy Strategy which has been recently introduced in England. Some help is also given to aid staff in identifying weak readers. The four basic developmental stages of reading are outlined and issues raised regarding the adaptation and differentiation of teaching materials. Some strategies are outlined relating to pupils with dyslexia.

Any teacher of pupils with SEN will inevitably come into contact with pupils who are weak readers, or even those who have virtually no reading skills at all. This can be a major problem for any teacher, from those who have considerable experience to those who are new to the profession. For many pupils described as having special educational needs in mainstream schools poor reading skills will be the crux of their difficulties. This chapter discusses some of the problems that can arise in this area and outlines possible strategies for teachers.

The National Literacy Strategy

The teaching of literacy to all pupils, particularly those of primary school age, has come under considerable scrutiny in recent years. The introduction of the daily literacy hour in 1998 has had a major impact on the way that literacy is taught and the organisation and management of lessons (Byers 1999).

The National Literacy Strategy Framework for Teachers (DfEE 1998a) describes the generic parts of the literacy hour as being essential elements to be covered on a daily basis with all pupils. However, despite the intentions described in the Green Paper, *Excellence for All Children: Meeting Special Educational Needs* (DfEE 1997a) to address SEN issues in all education initiatives, the *Literacy* document makes little reference to children with SEN. Beyond the key teaching strategies outlined in the *Strategy Framework* (DfEE,1998a, p. 8) there is little in it to help teachers with children with SEN in their classes.

As a result of an initial dearth of ideas described in the *Strategy Framework*, further guidance for use with children with SEN was produced. The intention of *The National Literacy Strategy Framework for Teachers (Additional Guidance) on Children with Special Educational Needs* (DfEE 1998b) is to identify some useful classroom strategies for teachers. The *Additional Guidance*, although largely general by nature, nevertheless reinforces good classroom practice for encouraging the development of literacy. The additional section identifies 'two broad groups of pupils' who might have special educational needs during the literacy hour (p. 113). One of the groups is those children described as having only minor difficulties in learning, while the other group is described as having severe and complex learning difficulties.

The group described as having only minor difficulties is seen as those who have difficulties with literacy as a result of being disadvantaged by their social background or their experiences of school. The focus of teaching for this group is described as being to help them catch up with their peers as quickly as possible.

The other group, with severe and complex learning difficulties, is seen as containing children more likely to have long-term difficulties. As such, the guidance states this group may be unable to work at the same pace and level as some of their peers and are more likely to need different teaching strategies. Furthermore, the section tells us that some of the children with severe and complex learning difficulties may be working at a level below that identified as being appropriate for their age group in the National Curriculum. To help alleviate this problem the DfEE and QCA have recently developed scales of criteria that will allow schools to set appropriate targets for the children who might fall into this category.

The *Additional Guidance* provides guidance that is set out in two categories, as general and specific points. The general issues include the following familiar points.

- The importance of adapting questions to meet the different levels at which pupils are working, along with developing effective reading strategies and giving explicit instructions, as well as reinforcing key teaching points.
- How extra classroom support, such as teaching resources and staffing, might be most effectively provided.
- The need for some children having difficulties with the literacy hour to have extra activities set up for them to meet their targets and how this should best be managed. The extra guidance points out that, in order to allow these children to participate in some of the activities with their classmates, time given to extra activities should be limited.

The specific guidance includes the following points.

- When the 'Big Book' is being used some pupils with SEN may be usefully served if extra copies are available. This, it is suggested, may help concentration.
- It is suggested that with whole-class focused word or sentence work some children may have difficulties with concentration and that appropriate activities as well as support and questioning techniques will prove useful towards aiding participation and concentration.

- When the focus is on group and individual work, the *Additional Guidance* points out the importance of appropriate grouping for children. This will allow them the opportunity to best use their abilities, allow them to use other children within their group as suitable role models and for their teachers and others helping them to focus on their individual needs.
- For the whole-class sessions the *Additional Guidance* emphasises the importance of giving time to allow children to reinforce, review and reflect on their learning. This approach, it is suggested, will not only help them to understand but also actively participate in understanding how the work they have done in the four parts of the literacy hour link together.

The *Additional Guidance* emphasises the need for teachers with children with SEN in their class to follow the pattern set out in the *Framework Strategy* and to take into account its relevant objectives in order to set suitable targets for children. In relation to children who have an IEP, the *Additional Guidance* emphasises the importance of making clear how adult support is to be used and provides details of any additional resources and adaptations that are to be used. It also stresses the importance of children with SEN being given the opportunity to practise the knowledge and skills they have learned in the literacy hour across the whole curriculum and in the wider school environment. The rest of this chapter focuses on strategies to help teachers to develop their knowledge and skills in this area of their work.

Recognising weak readers

There are certain tell-tale signs that can help a teacher determine if pupils have difficulties with reading (and following from this, the allied skills of writing and spelling). These signs commonly include:

- letter confusion (particularly b, d, p);
- reversals, e.g. 'was' for 'saw';
- difficulties in keeping pace with the rest of the class;
- a tendency to go from right to left rather than from left to right across the page;
- a failure of memory (particularly short-term memory);
- failure to use punctuation properly in what is read;
- an inability to build up unknown words by using the sound of the letters;
- an inability to use contextual cues and clues in reading to make sense of it;
- failure to make sense of phrases and sentences;
- poor speech patterns.

Reading difficulties can start with children having problems recognising the names and sounds of the letters in the alphabet. Many capital and small letters in our alphabet are visually very different (e.g. h and H, or g and G). For some pupils, for whom visual discrimination is a problem, this can create a major learning difficulty and may take many months or even years to sort out sufficiently for them to learn to read.

This is a situation that is further compounded when the individual letter sounds are combined into groups of two or three. Letter combinations like these make 108 different and recognisable sounds in the English language. Some of the combinations make accessible sounds while others are not used as part of our speech and writing. Examples of this include bl (as in black) or sch (as in school) while tj or fw are not to be found together in normal English usage. It is the problems of the English language such as these that pupils with special educational needs often find difficult to recognise.

The stages of reading development

Reading skills are developmental and as part of the process of learning to read three elements need to be addressed. These are: word attack skills, fluency, and comprehension skills. Children, as their reading develops, pass through several developmental stages. These stages can, in the simplest of terms, be equated with reading ages. This is a concept, discussed earlier, which gives some indication of the level of reading ability of children and is often used in comparison with the chronological age of the child. Thus a child with a reading age of nine and a similar chronological age will be at an average level in reading skills for this age. Children who are eleven and a half years old, and who have a reading age of eight years, would not only be well below the expectancy for the age group but also would need extra help to develop their reading skills to a level where they could cope adequately with the work with which they will be presented.

Pumfrey (1991), Reason and Boote (1994) and Westwood (1993) indicated there are various stages of competent reading development. Essentially these can be detailed in a four-stage model.

Stage One (reading age less than about seven and a half years). At this stage the child is still mastering the most frequently used words which make up the language. Examples of these are provided in the Dolch Word List (Dolch 1954). Children who are still at this stage of development in the upper primary and secondary school age group will have a poor vocabulary, have considerable difficulties in remembering what has been taught to them, and will need constant revision and reinforcement of work which has been done with them. At this stage children will have few or no phonic skills and will probably have learnt words that they can read by sight.

Stage Two (reading age about seven and a half to nine and a half years). This stage of development occurs when children begin to learn the rudimentary aspects of phonics (the sounds which make up most reading). As outlined earlier, there are 108 letter combinations that form the recognisable sounds of the language. Some are two-letter combinations such as 'sh' or 'th', while others are three or four-letter digraphs such as 'ould'. During this stage some children will start to develop the skills necessary to recognise some of these sounds while work will continue to be needed to develop skills and knowledge of the others. At this stage, for those children with difficulties in this area constant revision and practise will be needed.

Stage Three (reading age about nine and a half to eleven and a half years). It is at this stage that the more complex sounds are being mastered. It is also at this stage that a child will begin to break down the sound combinations in longer words to make them more manageable to read. This is a very important developmental skill and work at this level of operation needs to concentrate on the meaning of words and the development of vocabulary as well as the reading skills.

Stage Four (reading age about eleven and a half years upwards). At this stage all the fundamental work on the constituent parts of reading development are in place and children will have the necessary skills to tackle most of the words in the language. By this time difficulties in reading will be dependent on knowledge of vocabulary and interpretation of contextual meaning as much as anything else. Children at this stage of their reading development will usually receive help in their normal English lessons.

There is a considerable literature available on the teaching of reading from which further information on a variety of aspects can be gained. Pumfrey (1991) provides not only useful ideas on tasks for developing skills but also some background information on the neurological issues involved. For children at Key Stage 2, Reason and Boote (1994) and Moore and Wade (1995) offer a wide range of strategies for working with pupils who are experiencing difficulties in mainstream schools, while Westwood (1993) provides useful strategies specifically for children with SEN.

Helping children with reading

Increasingly as pupils move through school their ability to read will develop. There is so much diversity of progress that by the time children reach the secondary school there are likely to be pupils across the complete range of reading stages in a mixed ability class. Some of these will need only time spent with them and for someone to hear them read in order to alleviate their problems, while others will need long-term help.

The following are activities that may be used at each of the first three stages detailed above. Some of them are more appropriate for individual or small group situations as opposed to a large class environment. It is best to experiment and see what works best for you.

Stage 1
- Teach the child the letters of the alphabet; both the names of the letters and the individual sounds they make. In the light of comments made earlier check on those known and concentrate on a system that includes reinforcement and repetition to ensure knowledge and progress. Use flash cards where necessary. Watch out for 'pitfall letters': those that look alike – a kinaesthetic approach may be helpful here.
- Get the children to trace round dotted letters or simple words.
- Use basic word lists to concentrate on these. As with the letters of the alphabet, ensure constant revision and check knowledge.

- Produce flash cards to aid memory and use as a game with rewards for good work.
- Fill in missing letters or phonic sounds in words or sentences. Concentrate on letters or phonic sounds being taught.
- Ask simple questions from a passage of writing to check understanding. Use the answers to promote discussion.
- Underline words in a passage of writing.
- Point to particular words or sounds in a selection.
- Look for sounds at the beginning of a word. Play games like 'I spy'.
- Look for similarities in sounds and words. Do work on rhymes.
- Write down what the child says and make a booklet from it. Use illustrations from magazines or books to ensure it is about a topic of their choice. Get the student to read back what you have written.
- Use letter or word bingo, with small rewards or prizes.
- Play hangman.

Stage 2
- Use colour to highlight the particular sound or sounds being worked on.
- Work on basic sounds. Cover all 108 sounds to ensure they are known and remembered.
- Dictate short sentences of a specific sound (no more than five or six words).
- Use jumbled words or jumbled sentences to be rearranged by the pupils. Give lots of help here, some pupils find this exercise very hard.
- Add an end to a sentence. Keep the number of words required short and simple.
- Give comprehension exercises. Produce work cards for the pupil's use on topics of interest.
- Try simple spellings. Use words that are known to the pupil, e.g. those in basic vocabulary lists.
- Use the alternative word approach, e.g. 'The fate/fat man was on the bus'.
- Put circles around correct sounds in a passage of reading.
- Select correct spellings from a list of alternatives.
- Use punctuation exercises.
- Use of simple crosswords.
- Use matching words or matching sound exercises.
- Answer questions on a topical event.
- Promote reading for interest. Try shared reading among a group of children or perhaps a paired reading scheme with better readers in the class or in the school.

Stage 3
- Use colour to highlight the particular sound or sounds you are working from.
- Match words in sentences and passages.
- Use comprehension questions. Use the full range of question types, to encourage deductive skills.
- Work on form filling and letters of application. This is particularly useful with older pupils in their last years at school.
- Break down longer words, e.g. 'em ploy ment' or 'hes it ant'.

- Use Cloze procedure exercises.
- Conduct spelling exercises to build up known words. Use patterns where words are similar to build on.
- Use dictionaries to look up words and check spellings.
- Ask questions on things read from all sources of reading. Use items of interest to the child.
- Read together; short plays with a small number of parts or short stories.
- Develop punctuation skills. Concentrate on the basics: full stops, capital letters, sentences.
- Work on elementary grammar; nouns and verbs in particular.

Adapting reading resources

Adapting reading material for the less able in the class is an important form of differentiation for pupils. This particularly lends itself to differentiation by the tasks set for different pupils as well as by outcome through the way the different tasks might be assessed. To do this skilfully there are a number of important factors to be taken into account. The most important of these is the readability level that the child can cope with. This can be found out through the use of readability tests that are available and can be linked to the school computer. Some of these are complex in explanation and a handbook or the expertise of another member of staff can be invaluable here. A second, and more usual approach, is based on trial and error. Here the basic questions are:

- Can the children read it?
- Can they understand it?
- Is it interesting?
- Can they work from it?

Beyond these points a number of other considerations about the adaptation of teaching materials are worthwhile. These include:

Preliminary considerations
- Is the worksheet one of a series of multi-level sheets to be used with a mixed ability group? Is it to be used independently or with small groups? What is the range of ability of the users and how can this be catered for in relation to the content, presentation and readability of both the sheet and the tasks that are set?
- Is the worksheet aimed at promoting enquiry, testing previously taught information, and practising skills or other aims? Take into account the need to consider any combination of the aims suggested above – this will have an impact on presentation.
- Is a worksheet the best way of carrying out the tasks? Consider some of the alternative approaches: the use of the whiteboard, overhead projection sheets (if they are simple and clear), cassette recordings or class or whole-group lessons. Which approach will be the simplest and most effective? Can any of these be used in conjunction with a worksheet?

- How much will a worksheet cost? How many copies will be required? Will it be reusable?
- Is the worksheet to be evaluated and revised, if necessary? How will this be done? Is this the correct approach? How difficult will any changes be to make? Is there room for an input from the pupils (their judgement can be of great value)?

Writing and design

There are a number of points in the area of the writing and design of worksheets that must be considered.

- The language content must be appropriate for the target group. Look at the words you have used. Are they consistent with the most used and most easily read in the language? How long are the sentences (in this respect the shorter the better)? Are the sentences too complex (the best approach is one idea per sentence only with no subordinate clauses)? What technical vocabulary must I use, what can I do without to make it simpler?
- Beware of over complex or unknown vocabulary, over complex sentences, too large blocks of print, the overuse of capital letters, the extended use of personal pronouns and columns of print which are too complex for the children to deal with. The essential message is keep it simple.
- Look at the amount of information on each sheet. Is there too much? Would it be better if there were more than one worksheet to cover the information to be given? Don't make it too long.
- Are the instructions clear and precise? Do the pupils understand the terms I have used? Could I make them simpler?
- Are the drawings or diagrams simple for the pupils to follow? If photographs have been used do they come out clearly on the copies for the pupils; if they have not, should they be used or would they be best left out?
- Consider the layout and the positioning of the questions or tasks involved. Where is the best place for them in the text? Basically there are four positions: at the beginning of the text, at the end of it, in the middle or throughout it. Select whichever position serves the needs of the children most appropriately. It is important to explain to the group the aims of the worksheet. This may help them overall and give them some idea of what is being expected of them.
- Match the ability of the pupils and their interests to the tasks they are required to do. Consider the appropriateness of the tasks in relation to the work they can produce and the level of skill and motivation they have.
- Look at the number of tasks they are required to do and the variety of skills they will need to use. These tasks can include comprehension questions of both the factual or inferential types. (In the light of the overall ability of the pupils the balance between these types is important, with the accent for the less capable being on the factual/recall format).
- Other tasks can be multiple choice or Cloze type questions, illustrations, labelling diagrams, summaries in either words or pictures, one word or short phrase completion answers or developing or discussing points through small group discussions.

- Do allow enough space for the pupils to write (or draw) their answers. A cramped worksheet can be a very unrewarding experience for any child. It is important to remember that often the writing of pupils with special needs can be larger than some of the rest of their peer group.

Production

Consider the best type of reproduction that is available in the light of the following:

- the general appearance of the document;
- the spacing of the information on the page;
- breaking up the text with headings or titles to aid the weaker reader;
- the size of the print (remember in particular the needs of those with poor sight): it is also important to look at variations on the size of the print; this can make reading the text more interesting for the pupils and also help to emphasise the more important parts of the sheet;
- the use of coloured paper to coordinate worksheets of a similar theme or on a similar topic: think also about the use of coloured pens to emphasise points;
- underlining key words or phrases to emphasise their importance;
- numbering paragraphs or lines in the text to help those with reading difficulties to find the answers easily;
- if the worksheet is handwritten, is the text legible and is the prose style both easy to read and clear in intent to the pupil?
- try printing it broadways so that folded it will fit into an exercise book more easily: in this respect ensure the sheets are stuck into the exercise books or placed into folders when completed, without this they will fall out of the books and get lost.

Presentation

Consider reading the worksheet out aloud for the class. This will certainly help the weaker readers as well as perhaps motivating some of the pupils. Think about presenting the worksheet to some pupils by means of a tape recorder which they can control themselves and which allows a degree of independent learning. Another useful idea is to talk about any unfamiliar words or phrases before setting the children the piece of work (as mentioned above these words can be highlighted as a further prompt in the worksheet).

Further reading

Berger, A. and Gross, J. (1999) *Teaching the Literacy Hour in an Inclusive Classroom: Supporting Pupils with Learning Difficulties in Mainstream Education.* London: David Fulton Publishers.

Westwood, P. (1993) *Commonsense Methods for Children with Special Needs* (2nd edn). London: Routledge.

CHAPTER 10

Developing spelling and handwriting skills

Introduction

Reason and Boote (1994) argued that handwriting can be effectively used to support spelling with children with SEN. Bearing this in mind the development of spelling and handwriting will be taken together in this chapter.

Spelling

Spelling is regarded with great importance in society. A high value is placed on the ability to spell by certain elements of society; particularly employers who often associate poor spelling with carelessness. Good spelling has high status in school and is seen as a key factor in discriminating between the levels of skills held by pupils. In this respect it tends to be seen as a characteristic rather than a set of skills which can be learned.

For those pupils who have learning difficulties their spelling can be placed on a continuum from non-existent to having some difficulties with particular words. However, it can be a source of considerable anguish and concern. It is the intention in this chapter to consider the best approach to teaching spelling skills. This will concentrate particularly on the work done by a number of experts in this area (Peters 1985, Peters and Cripps 1983, Mushinski-Fulk and Stormont-Spurgin 1995a, b and Reason and Boote 1994).

Some children seemingly have no difficulties with spelling, while others have considerable problems. There is not a strong relationship between the ability to spell and general intelligence, nor is there always a clear relationship between spelling and the ability to read. Some good readers find that they are significantly weaker at spelling. However, as there is a close link between spelling skills and phonic knowledge, it is not likely that a weak reader will be good at spelling. In that sense at least there is a clear connection.

The evidence indicates that as with so many other skills admired and encouraged by the school, good spelling can be related to home background. This Peters (1985) indicated is certainly the case with children up to the age of nine. Cripps (1983) pointed out that better spellers have home environments where they hear conversations, have stories read to them, are good at games which encourage discrimination, have a good visual memory, are able to write quickly and neatly, where their letter formation is accurate, and use a continuous script.

Perhaps surprisingly, evidence collected indicates that the errors that pupils make are generally in only one part of the word, usually in the middle or at the end of it, and these errors often involve only one incorrect letter in the word. In an analysis reported by Peters (1985) it was ascertained that in a group of underachieving children aged 9 to 11 some 46 per cent of errors could be related to the confusion and substitutions of letters. Some 23 per cent related to letter omissions and 13 per cent to the transposition of letters. As with reading difficulties, the evidence indicates that spelling errors are often based on incorrect speech habits.

Why spelling is so difficult for some pupils

Peters (1985) indicated that there were four reasons for poor spelling. These are:

- Good spellers have a good internalised spelling system. This can be compared with a musician who can play from memory. This is a facility that is of great benefit to those who have it but is not a gift that all of us have.
- Spelling difficulties are compounded by the tendency of schools and society at large to over-emphasise its importance in written work and to take little or no account of the real situation of those who do not have a good internalisation system.
- Children are too often asked to write when the circumstances are not purposeful and because of this there is little need for them to produce writing with a high degree of legibility and correctness in order to communicate with others.
- Spelling is made more difficult by the way it is taught. Despite what we may expect, learning to spell is not the same as learning to read. Whereas some 80 per cent of sounds in learning to read are regular and provide little difficulty for the majority of pupils, spelling difficulties will occur with some of those words because of the different sound patterns within them.

Helping weaker pupils

Mushinski-Fulk and Stormont-Spurgin (1995a) advocated an interventionist policy for pupils with SEN. Undertaking such an approach (and bearing in mind the recommended time of one hour to one and a quarter hours each week for instruction (Pressley *et al.* 1990), their research indicated that this approach led to an improvement rate of over 90 per cent.

In a survey of appropriate techniques, Mushinski-Fulk and Stormont-Spurgin (1995b) identified a variety of approaches to the development of spelling for pupils with learning difficulties. An analysis of these shows that some are teacher-directed while others have a more student study focus. These approaches are discussed here in some detail.

Among the teacher-directed activities is the 'test–teach–test' approach. This is based on each session on spelling, which starts with giving the children a pre-test of the words to be worked with. The lesson focuses on those spelt wrongly at this point, with a final test to check on the progress made at the end of the session. In this way the lesson focuses only on the words spelt incorrectly at the beginning of the lesson.

Peters (1985) and Reason and Boote (1994) have argued that spelling should be allied to grammar, in that it is a form of communication that is concerned primarily with sequencing permissible combinations of words. Spelling is similarly concerned with the sequencing of permissible combinations of letters to make up words. In this respect Peters (1985) has argued that spelling should be taught through what she describes as 'letter strings'; combinations of letters which when placed together make certain sounds in the language. Various activities, which encourage the development of these skills, include:

- Finger tracing over letters in a word while a child simultaneously sounds it out. The importance of a multi-sensory attack is emphasised by this approach.
- Combining the teaching of spelling with the development of handwriting, which can also be taught in letter strings. Peters (1985) has argued there is a strong connection between good handwriting and good spelling.
- The use of 'letter string pockets' by pupils, where the word which the pupil had asked to be spelt is placed in the correct pocket for future use. This not only provides an aide memoir but also gives the pupil a multi-sensory, physical activity in an attempt to help them remember the position the string has been placed in.
- Peters and Cripps (1983) and Cripps (1983) proposed the use of the 'look–cover–write–check' technique. This approach involves the child in looking at the word in question, covering it up, writing it from memory and checking it for accuracy. There are various forms in which this can be undertaken including vocabulary books with folded pages or a procedure where the teacher writes the word on a piece of paper and the child has to carry it in their memory back to their place to write it down.

Reason and Boote (1994) argue that learning to spell is complex. They emphasise the need for encouragement, enjoyment and understanding in order for children to gain success. Furthermore, they point out the need for children to have a feeling of being a partner in controlling their development in this area.

Initial strategies suggested by Cripps, Peters, and Reason and Boote, indicate the importance of analysing the current work of children who appear to have difficulties. This can be done as a comparison between the level of ability of others in the class and, in the light of the experience of the teacher, the ability of children of a similar age.

A needs-analysis approach, relating particularly to the children's strengths, can be useful here. Factors to consider include what do the children already know and understand and at what stage are they in their personal development.

Reason and Boote (1994) detailed four stages in learning to spell. These equate roughly, not identically, with the first three levels outlined in the National Curriculum for English.

- Stage One relates to children who have the ability to recognise rhymes and rhyming words, have some ability to blend spoken sounds into words and who have some knowledge of the initial phonic structures in the writing of words.

- Stage Two is reached when children can write single letter sounds, some commonly used words of up to four letters and can analyse words into their constituent parts.
- Stage Three is reached when children can write words with consonant digraphs, consonant blends and vowel digraphs. At this stage they should also understand the use of the 'magic e' sound at the end of words and be able to spell most common words.
- At Stage Four children will be able to spell most words accurately and have developed skills in dictionary usage.

Children with weaknesses in spelling do not acquire skills incidentally. These skills need to be taught, and in many cases over taught, rigorously. Teachers will need to decide their priorities and work out their strategies to develop a systematic approach. A number of points need to be considered.

- What needs to be done with individuals, and what with the whole class? Sometimes certain general difficulties with a particular word or sound will emerge in a class. These can be dealt with collectively. When this occurs the use of a funny or odd explanation to underline the point can be very effective, as can the use of pictures. On other occasions the needs of children will be individual and will need to be tackled as such. Humour or some memorable approach may be useful to underline the points being made.
- A multi-sensory approach, using a variety of faculties may be appropriate for some children. This can be a very lengthy routine, but short cuts will not bring satisfactory results. The more obvious of these include listening properly to the word and its component parts, following the letters as each is said, writing or copying it down, memorising it and looking carefully at its difficult parts.
- The selection of words should be practical and useful to the child. The key words to be taught should give plenty of opportunity for use in their writing.
- The correction of spelling should be undertaken carefully so that the child is not faced with a myriad of errors and teacher corrections all over the page. One idea here is to focus on certain words. These could be those they are learning currently, those vital in the topic or subject area, or those considered to be key common words the child should be able to spell.

'Do's and Don'ts' in spelling

Peters and Cripps (1983) produced some simple instructions on this for the classroom teacher. They are reproduced here in simple form.

Do's
1. Talk with pupils about how words are constructed.
2. Tell them to look carefully at words and to think about the letter pattern, which is similar to those in words they know already.
3. Train them to visualise words with their eyes shut.
4. Teach them when learning a word to: 'look–cover–say–write–check'.

5. Make sure children always write from memory.
6. Write down words they have asked for and remove them before they attempt to write.
7. Help them with their handwriting.
8. Watch to see whether they are forming their letters properly.
9. Encourage them to be careful with their written work and to take a pride in it.

Don'ts
1. Allow learning to spell to become rote learning or an unpleasant chore.
2. Think that seeing a word is the same as looking carefully at it.
3. Let them copy from a sheet of spellings without going through the 'look–cover–say–write–check' sequence.
4. Spell out letter-by-letter words that have been asked for.
5. Let poor writers write too much on their own as free writing.
6. Allow them to form their letters incorrectly.
7. Get worried about 'slip-of-the-pen' mistakes.
8. Let them think they are poor at spelling.

Other activities and strategies to encourage good spelling

There are a number of activities and strategies that have been identified to aid teachers in developing spelling skills. Some of these can often be performed very effectively in small segments in a long lesson. Activities include:

- Use word lists reduced to manageable proportions for those with spelling difficulties. Bryant *et al.* (1981) argued that if a spelling list of 20 words is reduced to only four or five for some children this is much more manageable. A review of words learned in earlier lessons during the week helps to reinforce them.
- An approach called 'imitation plus modelling' is recommended by Mushinski-Fulk and Stormont-Spurgin (1995b). This approach involves the teacher spelling the word orally and children writing it. The word can then be checked. This is also done orally, with the teacher sounding out the individual letters of the word and either giving praise for a correct answer or writing the correct word.
- Mushinski-Fulk and Stormont-Spurgin also detail the 'constant time delay strategy'. This involves children spelling an appropriate word and then being shown the correct spelling. This is done a few times with what is described as a 'zero time delay'. The children observe the word during this process and are then asked to spell it again in a period of five seconds before it is shown to them again. Pupils then compare their spelling with the correct one. This is an activity that can be undertaken by pupils in pairs as well as being teacher-led.
- Use approaches which children can follow on their own or in small groups. Some of the approaches detailed here lend themselves to this, as do computer focused activities. There are an increasing number of computer-based games and approaches to help here. Check with other staff in the school or a publisher's catalogue to see what is available.

- Check that the children understand what rhyming words are and that they can use them.
- Use games. Finding words within words is particularly useful: for example, children's names (e.g. Richard = rich and hard) or place names (Manchester = man, chest, nest). Or use letter strings to make words: these can be taken from other words or from other sources such as suitable car registration plates. Communal hangman played on the board can also be a useful aid in spelling. Further ideas can be found in Reason and Boote (1994) and Westwood (1993).
- If a thematic approach is appropriate to the subject ensure there is an essential word list for the topic and that it is readily available for the class to use.
- Use what Peters (1985) described as 'rational correction techniques'. Get the pupils to look through their work and underline words they think they have spelled incorrectly: then concentrate on those they have missed. It is with this group of words that the children have a problem.
- For younger children the use of 'magic lines' as described by Reason and Boote (1994) can be helpful. This is useful when children cannot spell all of a word they wish to use; they make a line to indicate the parts which are missing or incomplete. Care is needed, however, to ensure that the number of incomplete words is not so large as to make the final piece too difficult to understand.
- Provide them with a wordbook or personal dictionary where they can write down key words. Use the 'look–cover–say–write–check' approach to this. This book can be used to construct tests for them.

The strategies include:

- Be positive about corrections. With poor spellers look for the words that are spelt correctly.
- Ask what the school or department policy on spelling is and follow it. Cripps (1983) argued that, at secondary level, without a school spelling policy, and it being given priority, pupil progress is unlikely. Furthermore, he contends that even with such a policy in place developing pupils' spelling will still be difficult and may be very time consuming.
- Point out difficult words in your own subject area.
- Allow children to participate in the selection of the list of words to be learned. This can increase motivation and allow them to feel they are part of the decision-making process.

There are a number of publishers' packages available to develop spelling skills. When choosing these it is important they relate to the age of the children and are age and task-appropriate. You should also feel comfortable as the teacher using the material. Publishers' catalogues are a useful starting point but much of this material, as with the equivalents in maths and reading development, is expensive.

Mushinski-Fulk and Stormont-Spurgin (1995b) have argued that whatever approach is used it is important that its purpose is explained to the children using it. The importance of personal effort to aid development should also be stressed, as should the tactic of the children practising the naming of the strategic steps of any approach they are using and the teacher carefully monitoring progress. Most importantly, they stress that whatever approach is adopted it will need a strong element of reinforcement for the pupils. Tangible reinforcements (such as stickers, merit cards or bar charts of progress) are strongly recommended whatever the approach used, as this can only help to motivate children.

Assessing spelling

Assessment, if used properly, can be a valuable tool to provide a sense of achievement for pupils as they develop their spelling skills. Informal assessments need to be targeted properly and clearly differentiated. This can be done in a number of ways. These include:

- limit the number of words given;
- grouping children, with appropriate words for each – include not only recently known words but unknown words;
- allowing the children to test each other on occasions;
- using individual progress charts to show personal development.

For some children appropriately differentiated short sentences may be dictated. This, as pointed out earlier, has major difficulties if not undertaken carefully. The Alpha to Omega series of exercises (Hornsby and Shear 1990) is a useful source for this.

For the more formal level of assessment, there are a number of published tests available. These include the Diagnostic Spelling Test (Vincent and Claydon 1981). This is a group test, basically for junior age children, which provides useful diagnostic information.

Dictionary work

For those children who are reaching Stage Four detailed by Reason and Boote (see earlier) there is value in dictionary work. The use of a dictionary is an aid to independence. However, to use a dictionary successfully children need certain skills. Some of these skills can be acquired only in the long term and for those at the early stages of developing these skills there is need of considerable reinforcement as well as practise of new skills. The basic knowledge required to undertake this work includes knowledge of the alphabet both in terms of letter order and individual location. For older children, a phonic dictionary that lists words according to their initial sound and syllable length, might be appropriate.

Handwriting strategies

Handwriting is often a problem for children with SEN. Those with poor motor control often have untidy presentation, which is unattractive to the reader and personally unsatisfactory to the children also.

There are a number of overall difficulties. Children often mis-form letters, start at the wrong point, and go the wrong way round when shaping them. Some have little skill in joining their letters together. As with spelling, learning handwriting is not incidental – it has to be taught with care and precision.

Handwriting changes with maturation and these changes can be noted particularly around adolescence; considerable changes in the size of letters and the way they are formed can occur. There can also be changes which can be accounted for in differences in the mood of children or the time of day. Tired children have a tendency to write less neatly.

A number of factors need to be taken into consideration in teaching children to write and in observing their work in this area. Alston and Taylor (1987) and Reason and Boote (1994) relate good handwriting to three key factors: legibility, fluency and speed.

Legibility

These include the physical conditions: the posture of the child, the positioning of the paper and the grip on the pen or pencil. The materials they are using are also a crucial factor. This includes the implement they are using. Here, the level of skill of the children should be the key factor rather than their age. The size and style of the paper also needs to be taken into account. Ruled paper is often very difficult for infants to work with. However, Reason and Boote suggest that for formal handwriting sessions even at that age ruled paper should be used. The size of a child's handwriting should also determine the width of the lines they are writing on. For some children with difficulties in keeping their writing in a straight line the use of guidelines under their paper or the page is encouraged.

Children should be encouraged to use tools that give the best results. The model of handwriting taught is also important. Alston and Taylor argued that those with poorer control should be taught cursive style as it is less demanding on them. There are indications that for many younger children with SEN poor control is a problem, and that printing continues to persist as a common approach. With older children though the cursive approach has advantages. It helps them to see words as a unit and can assist in the development of both fluency and speed as well as providing them with a more adult style. This is an issue that needs careful monitoring.

Good practice in this area needs careful planning. Short exercises in small groups are preferable, with close supervision by the teacher. The training and use of classroom ancillaries might be a possibility.

To develop good skills the children need to be carefully observed as they form their letters. Practise and praise are essential. Children should practise their letter formation by repeating the same letter along a line. Progress is best made by developing skills with letters of similar shapes, rather than in straight alphabetical order.

As with spelling, a multi-sensory approach can be useful in developing handwriting skills. Reason and Boote indicate that appropriate strategies include reading the letter, watching how it is formed, tracing round it with the finger and writing it out. They indicate that neither tracing nor simply copying letters is a sound tactic.

Fluency

Exercises to aid fluency include practising large rhythmic patterns on paper. The size of the paper needs to be commensurate with the needs of the children, moving from large to small paper with practice. Similarly finger tracing can be a useful exercise. For those with poor muscular control fluency can be improved by the teacher discussing with the child where they might place natural breaks in words they have written.

Speed

Speed improves with practice and in normal circumstances this should be sufficient. For some slower children practising letter strings may help here. Sometimes legibility and neatness may suffer as speed increases.

For pupils with a wide range of SEN both spelling and handwriting can present considerable difficulty. Particular and careful attention needs to be given to the teaching of these skills and teaching often needs to be done sequentially and with precision. It is important that these pupils are given both time and encouragement to develop their skills.

Further reading

Alston, J. (1999) *Developing Handwriting Skills*. Tamworth: NASEN.

Edwards, S. (1999) *Reading for All*. London: David Fulton Publishers.

Peters, M. (1985) *Spelling: Caught or Taught?* London: Routledge and Keegan Paul.

Pumphrey, P. D. (1991) *Improving Children's Reading in the Junior School*. London: Cassell.

Reason, R. and Boote, R. (1994) *Helping Children with Reading and Spelling*. London: Routledge.

Westwood, P. (1993) *Commonsense Methods in Special Education*. London: Routledge.

CHAPTER 11

Developing mathematical skills

Introduction

This chapter focuses on issues relevant to the teaching of maths, particularly basic arithmetic skills, to pupils who have considerable difficulties in this area of work. These difficulties, for many pupils and especially those with learning difficulties, can be related to the essentially conceptual nature of the subject. Children with SEN are easily confused by what is required by the processes of maths and may have little sense of what is expected to answer questions which have been posed. For these pupils even the apparently simplest of arithmetic tasks can be at a level which they find difficult without any form of tactile aids.

Issues covered in this chapter include the main problems pupils with SEN face in this area of the curriculum and suitable approaches which will help, and an outline of an appropriate model of good practice for the teacher is provided, particularly in the light of the recent introduction of the National Numeracy Initiative.

The National Numeracy Strategy

The National Numeracy Strategy (NNS) was introduced in 1999 as an initiative to raise numeracy skills among primary school children. As with the Literacy Strategy, introduced a year earlier, the NNS was based on a daily routine of good classroom practice in teaching mathematics.

It was suggested that good classroom practice centred largely on whole-class activities, particularly at the beginning and end of lessons. However, the National Numeracy Strategy stated that teachers must, as one of their duties, accommodate the flexibility, different timing, organisation and content within their lessons for both the most able and less able pupils. The aim of this initiative is to allow more children to reach a satisfactory standard.

The Task Force that developed the thinking on the NNS in the publication *The Daily Mathematics Lesson: Guidance for Professional Development* (DfEE 1999) asserted that the range of attainment in mathematics in many classrooms, particularly at the upper end of

Key Stage 2, is wide. The *Guidance* (p. 141) maintains that the introduction of this Strategy will reduce the number of children who have long-term problems with SEN. The document, while acknowledging the difficulties that might occur in the organisation and management of maths lessons, also indicates that all children who continue to need a Statement of SEN should participate in some part of the daily mathematics lesson with the rest of their peers. Similar to the guidance provided for the literacy hour, it is suggested that the middle part of the mathematics lesson (lasting some 30–40 minutes) is when children with severe difficulties in maths might follow a more individual programme of work and be given extra support.

Differentiation in maths

The DfEE (1999) advises that among those children who might find difficulty in keeping up with their peers in maths lessons are those who have three sorts of difficulties. These are short-term memory difficulties, difficulties in understanding mathematical concepts and difficulties in properly applying methods of calculation to obtain correct answers. The *Guidance* states that, although the structure of the numeracy hour envisages that all children in a class will work on the same topic at the same time, it will also be necessary to ensure there is a degree of differentiation for some children. The rest of this chapter will focus on strategies to help classroom teachers.

Difficulties

Mathematics often appears as an abstract, symbolic subject and Haylock (1991) has described teaching it to weaker pupils as 'one of the most difficult jobs in the world'. Nevertheless, as he also points out, it is a subject where this group of pupils can gain success and confidence. However, this may take place only slowly, over a long and sometimes frustrating period of time.

The Cockcroft Report (1982) supported the views of Piaget and others with regard to the different rates of development of pupils in attaining skills in maths. This suggests that there is a wide variation of skill, with some 11-year-old pupils being able to perform tasks expected of the average 14-year-old. However, others of that age are unable to perform the tasks expected of 7-year-olds.

The reasons for this disparity are based on a wide range of factors, and are dependent on the circumstances of the individual child. These can be related to cognitive or perceptual difficulties (where the concepts are too difficult for children to fully understand), poor manipulative skills, restricted concrete experiences in the concepts and ideas being taught, and breaks in the continuity of their learning, in what is essentially a sequential process.

It is this that makes it so important that the subject content for those pupils with difficulties should be clearly differentiated from that expected of their counterparts, and that account is taken of both the difference in the pace at which pupils with SEN can learn and their lack of ability to conceptualise or to work in abstract terms. Mathematics demands this and for some pupils their lessons, if the teacher is not careful, may be composed of a diet of the development of arithmetical skills only. This is a prospect that would not be helpful to either party.

There are a number of ways in which pupils with difficulties with maths can be identified. These include:

- Confusion in the meaning of the arithmetical signs. It is common among children who are weak mathematically at the age of 11 not to be able to recognise the division sign let alone be able to deal with the concepts involved.
- Visual sequencing problems of the numbers in the operation. Again it is common among this group of pupils in secondary school to be unable always to copy out a sum correctly.
- Inability to transfer from the horizontal presentation of work to be done to the vertical, and vice versa.
- Difficulties with place values, not understanding the difference between hundreds and thousands or even tens and hundreds.
- Conceptual weaknesses, not being able to give a rough estimate of an answer. This shows up particularly in calculator work when the answer is wrong and the child is unable to understand why.
- The inability to be able to transfer computational skills to real life situations. The reverse of this can also be the case when some practical situation demands arithmetic skills and the child is unable to understand which skill to use to find the right answer.
- Inaccuracies in working out answers. This can be a persistent problem or one that occurs occasionally. The first situation may be due to a lack of understanding of the skill needed; the second can often be due to a lack of concentration by the child or the child forgetting the skill required through a lack of internalisation on their part.
- Inaccuracies in presentation. A number of problems occur in this respect. These include poor handwriting and figure formation, which the child cannot follow, and the inability to set out the numbers in the question in the correct columns. Some children want to set out their work in the horizontal style and then find that they cannot work successfully in this mode. Pupils who are weak at arithmetic often need to write out the questions in vertical columns for greater accuracy.
- Poor vocabulary which will not allow the pupil to understand the question which has been asked.
- The readability level of the problem is too great and the child is unable to understand the language of the questions being asked. The maths skills of pupils with considerable reading difficulties may not be extended if they are constantly put in situations where the reading demands are too great for them.
- A poor attention span. Maths is a difficult area for concentrated effort for some pupils and for those who find the subject difficult this is an additional problem.

It is important to encourage good work habits in children and to develop their interest and competence in the subject through developing their confidence. It is vital that negative attitudes are not allowed to develop. This not only hinders development but also causes further behavioural difficulties.

Assessing maths skills

As with the assessment of reading skills described in Chapter 9, the assessment of mathematical skills can take two forms: formative and summative. This section concentrates on diagnostic and formative assessments.

Sellinger (1994) argued that the effective testing of mathematical skills must reflect, encourage and support pupil learning. Essentially diagnostic testing must elicit from pupils:

- their level of understanding of work which has been completed;
- problems they have encountered;
- information to help in the planning of future work.

Assessing the level of mathematical skills of children with SEN is often circumspect. It is usual that this takes the form of undertaking particular tasks in a specific context and relating this to what the children have already learned.

Sellinger argued that to assess the skills of children in this subject a wide range of approaches is valuable. She indicated these should include: listening, observing, questioning, discussing and interpreting the activities of pupils. This can be done either informally or formally.

Informal assessment

Informal assessments can be very useful to maths teachers. They can show the current knowledge of children (in terms of both their strengths and weaknesses) and help to find the correct starting point for them in a topic. Furthermore, they can be conducted in an unthreatening way, which will not only prove to be more accurate but also help to boost confidence.

Such assessments can take a variety of forms. However, it is important that they are set around appropriate tasks based on what the children have been taught. They can be knowledge-based, practical (such as survey work or working with shape or area), problem-solving, or a combination of all of these. The answers can be written, oral or aural or a combination of these approaches. They can be directed by the teacher or undertaken as an essentially pupil-centred activity.

In respect of the work of Piaget, discussed in Chapter 7, it is important to be able to ascertain at what level of mathematical thinking the children are working. In many cases for children with learning difficulties this will be at the initial concrete operations level of thinking, where they will be needing to deal in real terms with arithmetic issues. This may include the use of Cusinaire Rods, fingers or a number line to find the answers to questions.

The key points in any assessment of difficulties relate to:

- What did the child get wrong?
- Why did they get it wrong?
- Is it a problem of perception of how to address the task?

- Can children complete the task with the use of concrete examples?
- Can children explain the process that they are required to follow? At which point are they not able to do this?

Key levels of assessment

Westwood (1993) provided a series of key steps for assessing children's mathematical skills. These, if undertaken by the teacher, will indicate the level of attainment of pupils and provide a starting point for teaching. These are arranged in three levels of ability.

The first level concentrates on pre-number, vocabulary and number recognition work as well as the elementary aspects of arithmetic skills such as working with addition and subtraction skills with numbers of less than 10.

The second level deals with issues such as addition, simple mental arithmetic tasks with numbers under 20, and the use of both the vertical and horizontal setting out process for calculation as well as issues of telling the time and knowledge of the days in the week and months in the year.

The third level of assessment deals with pupils who have somewhat higher order skills. These include competences in the use of numbers beyond 100, knowledge of multiplication tables, understanding of place value, fraction recognition (in both the vulgar and decimal form) and satisfactory knowledge of working with both money and simple written problems.

Formal assessment

Formal diagnostic assessments in maths for pupils with SEN will provide either an overall quotient of ability or a profile of skill attainment. For those pupils with SEN it is often the latter of these that is the most useful and revealing.

The former type, such as the Maths 7–11 series (NFER 1990) may be useful to provide some indication of performance when compared with national standards or as part of the setting process for the maths department in a secondary school. However, this type of assessment will not always indicate the level of skills known by the child and as such will not provide the starting point at which teaching should begin. Tests which will do this include the Profile of Mathematical Skills (France 1979). As with reading tests, mathematics tests need to take into account the actual age of the children completing them.

Working within the National Curriculum

The National Curriculum specifies very clearly what children, unless they have been disapplied, are expected to work on. The list is wide ranging and includes measuring, weight, capacity, shape and area, and fractions. More detail can be gained from looking at the relevant sections of the National Curriculum documentation.

The non-statutory guidance from the National Curriculum Council (1989) provided guidelines on the approaches which may be appropriate. These include:

- balancing activities between those of a short-term duration and others where there is scope for longer-term work;
- ensuring that the activities are balanced between independent and cooperative work;
- setting tasks where there is a balance between exact results and many possible outcomes;
- employing different approaches to learning: these include observations, talking and listening, discussion with other pupils, reflecting on activities completed, drafting, and reading and writing;
- ensuring that pupils are able to develop their personal qualities; and
- activities which enable the pupils to develop a positive attitude to maths.

Classroom management strategies

There are a number of models (Bailey 1982, Haylock 1991, Aherne 1993) which indicate appropriate approaches for pupils with SEN, particularly those with learning difficulties. That provided by Bailey is a particularly useful overall approach. He argued that any approach must take into account the following issues:

- *defining* the aims and objectives for the pupils in the lessons;
- *assessing* the pupils, using a variety of different approaches including normative and criterion-referenced material, informal observations and error analysis;
- *planning* the teaching programme and present learning experiences through a range of materials, strategies and organisational features;
- *evaluating* the teaching programme through ongoing assessment of pupils' progress.

Providing help

For pupils with difficulties in maths Westwood (1993) argues for a balanced approach to teaching, where there is a considerable focus on explicit teaching accompanied by 'hands-on' experience. He further argued that the discovery method and both group and collaborative learning approaches are less efficient for those with difficulties in this subject.

Ablewhite (1969) indicated there are key principles to be taken into consideration when teaching maths to weaker pupils. These are related to pace, awareness, vocabulary, the concept of number, motivation, presentation, readability and vocabulary.

Pace

Children learn at different speeds and in different ways. With this in mind teachers must provide useful and enjoyable tasks rather than setting predetermined goals to be met by the end of the term. It is also important that pupils are not allowed to become bored. Westwood points out the importance of teacher awareness concerning the pace with which material is presented to a child so that the child can assimilate the skills and concepts properly before moving on to new material.

Awareness

Ensure that the children are properly aware of what they have been doing. This will help them to remember more clearly the things they have learned.

Vocabulary

Ensure that the child's vocabulary is developed to the point where there is a good understanding of the terms that are essential to both learning and understanding. Where there is a language deficiency work will need to be done in this area.

The concept of number

For children with SEN it is important to work on their concept of number and their basic arithmetic skills for a large extent of the time. However, do not expect progress to be quick. For many pupils with SEN the concepts of arithmetic, let alone mathematics, are a mystery and it may take a long and painstaking effort from both them and you before the 'fog' begins to lift. Westwood recommends the use of a revisiting approach with key teaching points being revisited and revised regularly.

Motivation

It is important in maths, as in other areas of the curriculum, that the contents of lessons help to motivate the children. This can operate in two clearly defined ways. Firstly, the pupils can see the content of lessons as directly relevant to their future needs on either a personal or social level. Since aspects of the maths curriculum clearly lend themselves very easily to this, it is important that this is used by the teacher whenever possible. Secondly, there are aspects of the maths curriculum that pupils find intrinsically interesting and will work at with considerable motivation. These aspects of course vary from child to child and it is an important part of the teacher's management skills to find out about their interests and to concentrate for a considerable proportion of their teaching time on these.

Presentation

When presenting work in maths to pupils with learning difficulties the layout of the material can be crucially important. An attractive page of work will serve to motivate children. Bearing this in mind it is important that the material should be presented attractively, perhaps with illustrations and diagrams. Small print should be avoided: this is not helpful to those with reading difficulties and can cause particular difficulties for pupils with sight problems. It is also important to avoid close spacing of lines and heavy blocks of written text as they are particularly off-putting to pupils with SEN.

Readability and vocabulary

Similarly, the question of the readability of the material is important. Pupils with difficulties in maths often have difficulties with reading and writing. It is important to avoid long, complicated sentences, uncommon words and multi-syllabic and irregular words. Time can be fruitfully spent on talking over the vocabulary of the text that is presented and also that of the instructions for completing the work and to check on any ambiguities that may arise.

Experience will indicate to the teacher which mathematical terms will cause the most difficulties; however, a good rule of thumb is explain and discuss fully any new terms which crop up. It is also a valuable exercise to look at the vocabulary which has been used and to see which, if any, could be simplified or omitted altogether.

The content of maths lessons needs to be kept simple. Bearing in mind all the points made above, children will easily be confused if there are complicated instructions or concepts to be handled and learned. It is important to remember that the number of variables that a child can handle is determined by their intellectual ability. Haylock (1991) suggested that for those pupils with SEN, maths should be taught in carefully sequenced stages.

Further reading

Berger, A., Morris, D. and Portman, J. (2000) *Implementing the National Numeracy Strategy for Pupils with Learning Difficulties: Access to the Daily Mathematics Lesson.* London: David Fulton Publishers.

Waugh, D., Stakes, J. R. and Hornby, G. (2000) *Broad, Balanced and Relevant: Meeting the Needs of Children with Learning Difficulties Within the National Curriculum.* Hull: Halfacrown Academic.

Westwood, P. (1993) *Commonsense Methods in Special Education.* London: Routledge.

CHAPTER 12

Working with parents

Introduction

Establishing constructive working relationships with parents is a key element of meeting the educational needs of all children but it is particularly important for those children with SEN. This is because parents of children with SEN are likely to require greater support and guidance than many other parents and also because there are many ways in which such parents can help teachers to provide the most effective education for their children. This chapter considers what teachers need to know and do in order to work in partnership with parents. First, a model for understanding different aspects of parental involvement is presented. Then, various strategies which teachers can use to establish and maintain effective communication with parents is described. This is followed by suggestions for facilitating parental involvement in assessments and reviews of progress. The final section of the chapter focuses on the listening skills, counselling skills and assertion skills which teachers need to develop in order to work effectively with parents.

A model for working with parents

A model which illustrates various aspects of parental involvement is presented in Figure 12.1. The model consists of two pyramids, one representing a hierarchy of parents' needs, the other a hierarchy of parents' strengths or possible contributions. Both pyramids demonstrate visually the different levels of needs and contributions of parents. Thus, while all parents have some needs and some potential contributions which can be utilised, a smaller number have an intense need of guidance, or the capability of making an extensive contribution. The model also shows that, for parents' needs at a higher level, more time and expertise is required by teachers in order to meet these needs. Each of the components of the model will now be outlined and teachers' roles in each of these discussed.

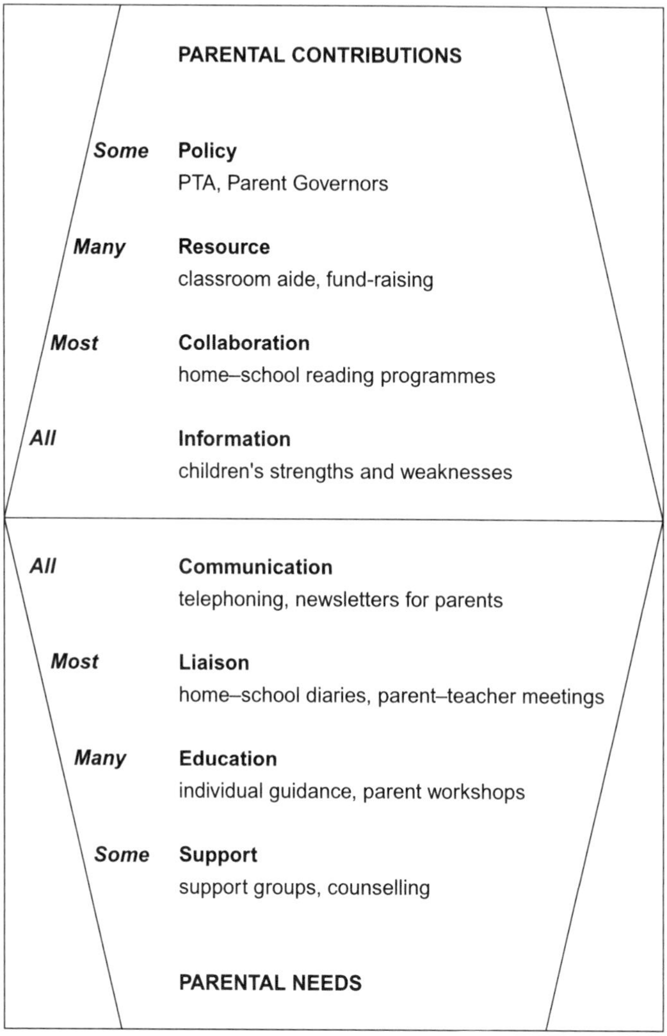

PARENTAL CONTRIBUTIONS

Some   **Policy**
PTA, Parent Governors

Many   **Resource**
classroom aide, fund-raising

Most   **Collaboration**
home–school reading programmes

All   **Information**
children's strengths and weaknesses

All   **Communication**
telephoning, newsletters for parents

Most   **Liaison**
home–school diaries, parent–teacher meetings

Many   **Education**
individual guidance, parent workshops

Some   **Support**
support groups, counselling

PARENTAL NEEDS

Figure 12.1   A model for working with parents

Needs of parents

Communication with parents

All parents need to have effective channels of communication with the teachers who work directly with their children. They need information about the organisation and require-ments of the school as it affects their children. They need to know how their children are progressing and about any assessments, reviews or changes of placement which are being considered. That is, all parents need to know about their rights and responsibilities. This can be provided through handbooks or regular newsletters written especially for parents.

Parents need to feel that they can contact the school at any time when they have a concern about their child. Some parents prefer to communicate by telephone, others would rather call in to see the teacher face to face, while others find that contact through written notes or home–school diaries suits them best. Therefore, teachers need to ensure that a wide range of communication options are open to parents. However, the most important factor in maintaining good communication is the openness to parents which schools demonstrate through their contacts with parents. The attitude of choice has often been referred to as an 'open door policy' in which parents feel comfortable about contacting or going into the school when they have a concern. The key element of this policy is the teacher's willingness to establish and maintain open communication with parents.

Liaison

Most parents want to know how their children are getting on at school. They want to find out what their children have achieved and whether they are having any difficulties. They regard teachers as the main source of information on their children's performance at school and therefore need to have a working partnership with them. Teachers can facilitate this by keeping in regular contact with parents through such means as telephone calls, home visits, home–school notebooks, weekly report forms and by meeting with parents at school (for a detailed discussion of these forms of liaison see Hornby 2000).

Teachers are often disappointed that some parents do not come to parent–teacher meetings at school, thereby giving the impression that they are not interested in how their children are getting on. However, there are usually other reasons for them not attending, such as the difficulties involved in getting a babysitter, the overwhelming demands of looking after their family, or anxieties about coming to the school which are related to their own negative school experiences. It is important then, for teachers to find other ways of liaising with these parents, perhaps by having regular telephone contacts or home visits.

Education

Many parents appreciate receiving guidance from teachers on promoting their children's progress or dealing with specific difficulties. In fact, they are much more likely to approach teachers, who are in daily contact with their children, than head teachers or educational psychologists who they may see as more threatening. Class teachers are in an excellent position to provide parents with such guidance. They are knowledgeable about child development and learning and see children on a daily basis, so have the chance to get to know them well and identify any changes in behaviour or difficulties in learning which they may experience. Therefore, opportunities for receiving such guidance, or what is in effect parent education, should be freely available to all parents.

A particularly effective format for parent education is one which combines guidance about promoting children's development with opportunities for parents to discuss their concerns. Parent education programmes which involve a group of parents, and employ a workshop format, easily lend themselves to providing a combination of educational input and sharing of concerns. This type of format, enables parents to learn new skills and gain confidence through talking to other parents and teachers.

Support

Some parents of children with SEN, at some times, are in need of supportive counselling, even though they may not actually request it. This support can be provided either individually by teachers, educational psychologists or social workers, or in groups such as self-help groups or support groups. Although such support should be available to all parents, the majority of parents seldom need extensive counselling. In the past it has often been assumed that the greatest need of parents of children with SEN is counselling in order to help them come to terms with their child's disability. This has led to an over-emphasis on this aspect of parent involvement to the detriment of the other aspects, such as communication and liaison, which have been discussed above. The fact is that if parents have good channels of communication and regular liaison with teachers, coupled with the opportunity to receive guidance about their children whenever they need it, then only a very few of them will need extensive counselling at any particular time.

Whereas most British parents are reluctant to seek the help of professional counsellors, they will approach their children's teachers in search of guidance or counselling for the problems which concern them. Teachers should therefore have a level of basic counselling skills sufficient to be good listeners and to help parents solve everyday problems (see Hornby 1994). They should also be able to refer parents on to professional counsellors or support groups when problems raised are beyond their level of competence.

Parents' contributions

Information

All parents can contribute valuable information about their children because they have known them throughout their lives and have been the ones who have participated in all previous contacts with professionals in order to assess and plan for meeting their children's needs. Information concerning children's likes and dislikes, strengths and weaknesses, along with any relevant medical details can be gathered by teachers at parent–teacher meetings. Many parents feel more comfortable on their own territory and generally appreciate it when teachers offer to visit them. This also provides an opportunity to observe how parents cope with their children at home and to learn about any relevant family circumstances. Making full use of parents' knowledge of their children not only leads to more effective teaching, it also makes parents feel that they have been listened to and that an active interest has been taken in their children.

Collaboration

Most parents are willing and able to contribute more than just information. Most parents are able to collaborate with teachers by reinforcing classroom programmes at home in activities ranging from checking homework diaries to conducting home–school reading or behavioural programmes. However, while involvement in such schemes should always be offered to all parents, including those who have not collaborated in the past, it should be accepted that a small proportion of parents will not be able to participate for a variety of justifiable reasons. The class teacher's role is to optimise levels of collaboration for the maximum number of parents.

Resource

Many parents have the time and ability to act as voluntary teacher aides, either assisting in the classroom or in the preparation of materials, or in fund-raising. Others may have special skills which they can contribute such as helping prepare newsletters, in craft activities, or in curriculum areas in which they have a special talent. In these times of contracting professional resources teachers should make sure that they make optimum use of this valuable voluntary resource. Therefore invitations to parents to help at the school need to be sent out at least annually by means such as newsletters.

Policy

Some parents are able to contribute their expertise through membership of parent or professional organisations. This includes being a school governor, a lay inspector, a member of the PTA, or being involved in a parent support or advocacy group. Others have the time and ability to provide in-service training for teachers. Parents can influence school policy on children with special needs through their involvement as a governor or PTA member. They can also sometimes influence Government policy on children with special educational needs through their involvement in groups such as MENCAP and SCOPE (formerly The Spastics Society). Therefore teachers should continually be on the look out for parents who can contribute in these ways so that their abilities can be used to the full.

Communicating with parents

There are five main methods for developing and maintaining two-way communication between parents and teachers. These are informal contacts, various forms of written communication, telephone contacts, parent–teacher meetings, and home visits. These are now discussed in turn, starting with informal contacts. Detailed guidelines for each of the five methods of communication with parents are described elsewhere (Hornby 1995).

Informal contacts

Typical forms of informal contacts are school productions which involve the child with SEN, open days, gala days, and educational visits in the community. Such informal contacts are a useful way of 'breaking the ice' in most forms of human relationships and this is also the case in relationships with parents. Such contacts provide a means whereby parents and teachers can meet each other as people with a mutual interest in building relationships on behalf of children, thereby helping to break down the barriers that often exist between school and home. Informal contacts are particularly important for parents of children newly enrolled at the school or when there has not been a high level of parent involvement at the school in the past. In the latter situation teachers understandably become despondent when the attendance at more formal events, such as parents' evenings, is so poor. When this is the case it is often best to organise informal events in order to increase the numbers of parents having contact with the school and thereby establish the context necessary for the development of other forms of contact.

Written communication

Many parents prefer to communicate with teachers by means of letters. Other parents find that home–school diaries are the best means of keeping in contact with the school. In addition, newsletters and handbooks written especially for parents of children with SEN can keep parents in touch with what is happening at school. Progress reports are also used to maintain communication with parents. It is therefore clear that the written word provides an important means of communication between teachers and parents.

However, there are two major difficulties with this form of communication. First, if some of the pupils' parents do not have English as their first language then ideally every written communication to parents needs to be translated into their own languages. Second, it is important to remember that some parents have reading difficulties themselves. Therefore, written materials cannot be relied upon to communicate effectively with all parents. This also suggests that all written materials should use language which is simple and able to be understood by the majority of parents.

Telephone contacts

Some parents prefer to communicate with teachers by means of the telephone. Many parents appreciate the opportunity of being able to phone teachers directly either at school or at home. However, there are difficulties associated with both of these options. The main problem with parents phoning teachers at school is that teachers should only have to leave their class to answer the telephone in absolute emergencies. So it is best to get the school secretary to take messages and tell parents that the teacher will phone back as soon as possible. Also, many teachers may not be prepared to allow parents to phone them at home. This is perfectly understandable since they may feel the need to have some time to themselves, or with their own families, which work pressures do not impinge on. An alternative solution is to set a specified time during the week when parents know the teacher will be available to answer the phone.

Alternatively, teachers may prefer to contact parents by telephone rather than by sending a letter. It is useful to check whether some parents are at home during the day and whether others are happy to be phoned at work, in which case such calls can be made from school during the day.

Parent–teacher meetings

The form of contact with parents with which all teachers are familiar is that of parents' evenings or parent–teacher meetings. These meetings are a well established method of involving parents and not without reason, as research has shown that they have an impact on both parent–teacher relationships and pupil progress. It has been found that children whose parents attend such meetings have higher attendance rates, fewer behaviour problems and improved academic achievement. Of course experienced teachers would immediately suggest that this is because the parents of 'good kids' usually attend parents' evenings whereas parents of pupils with behavioural or learning difficulties tend not to turn up. However, it must not be assumed that parents who do not turn up to parents' evenings are not interested in their children's education. There are a variety of reasons why some parents do not attend such meetings, including transport and babysitting problems, as well as parents' negative feelings about their own school days. Perhaps, if these problems could be overcome, these parents would come to parents' evenings, and this would lead to better parent–teacher relationships and thereby an improvement in their children's progress at school. I believe that it would, but it is usually easier to use other strategies to communicate with these parents to overcome the problems. By using either home visits, telephone contacts or written communication, good parent–teacher relationships can be established which should lead to improvements in children's behaviour and academic progress.

Home visits
Many parents appreciate it when their children's teachers are prepared to come and visit them on their own territory. Such home visits can be pivotal in establishing close working relationships with parents. They enable teachers to see for themselves the circumstances in which the family are living. They also enable teachers to meet other members of the family, such as siblings and fathers, who they may not otherwise meet. Knowledge of these factors can help teachers understand how their pupils may be affected by the home situation.

Home visits also enable teachers to find out how their pupils spend their time at home, whether they have any hobbies, how much television they watch and what time they usually go to bed. It is also possible to find out how pupils behave at home and how their parents handle them. Finally, home visits provide an opportunity for teachers to answer parents' questions and deal with any concerns they may have.

Parental involvement in assessments and reviews

The aspects of parental involvement discussed above are important in developing constructive working relationships between teachers and parents. In addition, a specific requirement of the *Code of Practice* is parental involvement in assessment of children with SEN and reviews of their progress. Parents must be included in the process of statutory assessments which may lead to Statements of SEN and must also be involved in annual reviews of Statements. Parents should also be involved in the assessment process required for the design and review of IEPs.

Wolfendale (1992) suggests that assessment should be conducted by means of a partnership between parents and teachers. In the early stages it should encompass the sharing of information, with both parents and teachers setting out their opinions and concerns about children. Later, more specific information on the child's development should be collected by parents and teachers by such means as observations, checklists and tests. The information collected is then shared in a parent–teacher meeting so that an assessment of the child's behaviour and attainments in both home and school settings is achieved. Viewing parental and teacher assessment information as complementary in this way leads to a more open sharing of perspectives and thereby promotes the development of a collaborative partnership.

Since involving parents in the assessment and review processes is likely to significantly improve the quality of information available it is important to attempt to optimise the effectiveness of parental involvement in these processes. That is, rather than parents being seen as recipients of information who are asked to comment on assessment results produced by teachers or others, they should be seen as active partners in the process of collecting and reviewing assessment data. Meetings with parents to discuss assessments and reviews of progress should therefore be conducted and every attempt made to ensure that, rather than feeling intimidated, they feel empowered to participate to the fullest extent. Suggestions on how this can be accomplished are discussed below.

Assessments

A variety of approaches have been used in attempts to improve the effectiveness of parental input into the assessment of their children (Wolfendale 1992). These have involved parents in the completion of diaries, observation charts, developmental checklists and parental profiles in order to assess the behaviour and development of children. Parental profiles have been used in situations as diverse as assessing children's progress prior to their entry into school as rising five-year-olds and preparing material to present as the parental advice required for statutory assessments.

The *Code of Practice* recognises the benefits of providing a structure for optimising written parental contributions to assessments and suggests providing parents with pro formas to guide their input into the assessment process. Such pro formas should be used for all assessments conducted with children who have SEN. They will need to be adapted for children of different ages or to suit the particular situation for which they are used but will generally include questions on the following aspects:

- Health: e.g. medical problems, medication taken;
- Physical development: e.g. fine or gross motor skills;
- Eye–hand coordination: e.g. threading, drawing, assembling;
- Self-help: e.g. dressing, handling money, travelling independently;
- Communication: e.g. clarity of speech, vocabulary, fluency;
- Basic academic skills: e.g. reading, writing, spelling, number skills;
- Work habits: e.g. concentration span, study skills, memory;
- Play/leisure: e.g. hobbies, sporting activities;
- Behaviour: e.g. over-active, nervous, defiant, moody;
- Relationships: e.g. with siblings, friends, adults.

Progress reviews

Pro formas have also been used to improve the effectiveness of parental input into reviews of children's progress (Hughes and Carpenter 1991). Forms should be devised for parents to fill in in order to help them organise their thoughts on their children's progress and needs so that they can contribute more meaningfully to reviews of IEPs or Statements of SEN. Pro formas should generally address the following areas:

- General health
- General behaviour
- Abilities
- Likes and dislikes

- Independence
- Priority areas
- Home circumstances.

Skills needed for working with parents

In order for teachers to work effectively with parents there are certain interpersonal skills which are needed. The most important of these are listening skills, counselling skills and assertion skills. These skills are outlined below and discussed in more detail elsewhere (Hornby 1994).

Listening skills

The major components of listening are attentiveness, passive listening, paraphrasing and active listening.

Attentiveness
Effective listening requires a high level of attentiveness. This involves focusing one's physical attention on the person being listened to and includes several components:

- maintaining good eye contact;
- facing the speaker squarely;
- adopting an open posture;
- leaning slightly forward;
- avoiding distracting body movements;
- maintaining a comfortable distance;
- remaining relaxed.

Passive listening
Passive listening involves a high level of attentiveness combined with other skills:

- invitations to talk, e.g. 'How can I help you?';
- neutral feedback, e.g. 'Go on', 'Right', 'Huh Huh';
- avoiding communication blocks, e.g. criticism or reassurance;
- giving the other person one hundred per cent attention;
- avoiding self-listening, i.e. not going off into one's own thoughts;
- using open questions for clarification or encouragement;
- using attentive silence in order to encourage parents to open up.

Paraphrasing
Paraphrasing is a skill which involves feeding back the main points of the message to the person for his or her confirmation. It has four components:

- the paraphrase feeds back only the key points of the speaker's message;
- paraphrasing is concerned with the factual content, not feelings;

- it is short and to the point;
- it is stated in the listener's own words but in familiar language.

Paraphrases are used when speakers are clearly wanting some response from the listener. At this point the listener feeds back the essence of the speaker's message and then waits for a response. When the paraphrase hits the mark speakers typically indicate that this is the case by saying, 'That's it' or 'Right' or 'Yes', or by some non-verbal means such as nodding their head. If the paraphrase is only partly accurate then the response will not be so positive and in most cases the speaker will correct the listener. In so doing speakers will also be clarifying for themselves exactly what is meant, so the paraphrase will still have been of value.

Active listening

Active listening involves trying to understand the key message and feelings and then putting this understanding into your own words and feeding it back to the person. Thus, active listening builds on attentiveness, passive listening and paraphrasing in that the main aspects of what is being communicated are reflected back to the person. The process of active listening involves reflecting both thoughts and feelings back to the speaker.

The speaker's key feeling is fed back, along with the apparent reason for the feeling. When teachers are learning how to use active listening it is useful to have a set formula to follow. The formula, 'You feel . . . because . . .' is typically used. For example:

- You *feel* frustrated *because* you haven't finished it.
- You *are* angry *about* what happened.
- *You're* sad *that* it has come to this.
- You *were* pleased *with* what they achieved.

However, active listening involves much more than simply using this formula. It requires listeners to set aside their own views in order to understand what the other person is experiencing. It therefore involves being aware of how things are said, the expressions and gestures used and, most importantly, of hearing what is not said.

Counselling skills

Being a good listener is often not enough. Parents need help in clarifying their problems and in establishing strategies to deal with them. What is needed by teachers who work with parents of children with SEN is a broader model of helping which includes listening but which enables them to go beyond this when circumstances demand it. In order to address this need a counselling model is proposed based on a general approach to counselling that is used with children and adults in a wide variety of situations.

Three-stage counselling model

The counselling model proposed involves a three-stage approach to counselling with stages of *listening*, *understanding*, and *action planning*. It is a problem-solving approach to counselling adapted from previous models by Allan and Nairne (1984) and Egan (1982) and is described in more detail elsewhere (Hornby 1994).

Parents of children with SEN are much more likely to be willing to talk about their concerns with someone who is working directly with their child, such as a therapist or teacher, than with a professional counsellor who they do not know. If teachers use listening skills with parents any concerns they have will emerge. Teachers should then be able to help by using basic counselling skills and being prepared to refer parents on for more intensive help when necessary.

The rationale for using such a model is based on the idea that the majority of problems, concerns or ideas which parents bring to counselling can be dealt with by taking them through the three stages of the model in order to help them find the solution that best suits their situation. First of all, the teacher uses the skills of *listening*, which were discussed above, to establish a working relationship with parents, to help them open up and to help them explore any concerns or ideas they have.

Next, the teacher uses the skills of *understanding* in order to help parents get a clearer picture of their concerns or ideas, develop new perspectives on their situation, and suggest possible goals for change. Summarising is used in order to help parents clarify their major concerns or ideas. Parents are then helped to develop new perspectives on their situations perhaps by teachers sharing from their experiences of working with children with SEN. Finally, to facilitate movement from stage two to stage three, parents are helped to develop realistic goals for solving their problems or implementing their ideas.

Then, the teacher moves on to *action planning*, in which problem-solving skills are used in order to help parents decide what, if anything, they want to do about their concern or idea. That is, to consider possible options for solving their problems or implementing their ideas. Parents are also helped to develop plans for action and assertively implement their plans. Finally, in subsequent sessions, parents are helped to review their progress in implementing their plans.

Possessing the skills required to use this simple three-stage problem-solving model of counselling will contribute enormously to the ability of teachers to establish productive partnerships with parents. Some of the skills required for the third stage of the model are discussed in the following section on assertion skills.

Assertion skills

Assertiveness involves being able to stand up for your rights while respecting the rights of others; being able to communicate your ideas, concerns and needs directly, persistently and diplomatically; being able to express both positive and negative feelings with openness and honesty; and, being able to choose how to react to situations from a range of options.

Teachers need assertion skills both for working with parents and for collaborating with other professionals. Teachers will need to make and refuse requests and will have to deal with criticism and aggression from time to time. They will also need to be able to give constructive feedback to parents as well as colleagues. Finally, they will need to be able to help both parents and colleagues to resolve conflicts and solve problems. The skills involved in these situations are outlined below and are discussed in more detail elsewhere (Hornby 1994).

Refusing a request

Teachers will sometimes receive requests from parents or colleagues which they think they should not agree to but feel unable to turn down. People have difficulty saying 'no' for several reasons, especially due to the fear that it will damage their relationship with the other person. The alternative to agreeing to requests you would rather turn down is to use acceptable ways of saying 'no', several of which are listed below.

- *The explained 'no'* – when you give a genuine reason for the refusal.
- *The delayed 'no'* – when you ask for time to think it over.
- *The listening 'no'* – when listening skills are used to show you understand.
- *The 'broken record' 'no'* – when you make a brief statement of refusal to the request and repeat this as many times as necessary (like a broken record) until the message gets across.

Making a request

Teachers sometimes need to request various things from their colleagues and parents. So, being able to make requests effectively is important, especially since many people find it difficult to do. Useful guidelines for making requests are outlined below (from Manthei 1982).

- State your request directly, firmly and clearly to the other person.
- Say exactly what you want – be specific and precise.
- Focus on the positive – create an expectation of compliance.
- Answer only questions seeking clarification – do not get side-tracked.
- Allow the person time to think about it.
- Repeat the request using the 'broken record' technique.
- Be prepared to compromise and realise the other person has the right to refuse.

Responding to criticism

A four-step model for responding to criticism is outlined below (from Holland and Ward 1990).

- Step one: listen carefully to the criticism.
- Step two: decide what is true and what is not.
- Step three: apologise for what is true and firmly refute what is not.
- Step four: learn what you can from the criticism and move on.

Dealing with aggression

When teachers are faced with aggressive behaviour they *should not:*

- argue with a person who is behaving aggressively;
- raise their voices or begin to shout;
- become defensive and feel they have to defend their position;
- attempt to minimise the concern which the other person is expressing;
- take responsibility for problems which are not of their making;
- make promises which they will not be able to fulfil.

All of these responses are commonly used by people confronted with aggression but they seldom work and are more likely to make the other person more aggressive. The following responses (from Kroth 1985) are far more likely to calm down the other person and lead to a constructive resolution of the situation. *Teachers should:*

- actively listen to the other person to confirm that you are listening;
- speak softly, slowly and calmly;
- ask for clarification when complaints are vague;
- make a list of the concerns;
- use the techniques of problem-solving, discussed below, to work through the list of concerns, starting with the one of highest priority to the other person.

Giving constructive feedback

Whereas criticism is generally given without intending to be helpful, constructive feedback is aimed at helping people to function better. A model for providing constructive feedback which has been found extremely useful is one adapted from the DESC script popularised by Bower and Bower (1976). This is a technique which teachers find valuable in giving feedback to parents of children with SEN and also to their colleagues and which, in addition, parents find useful in handling difficulties with professionals. DESC stands for: describe; express; specify; consequences. The four steps involved in using the modified DESC script are described below.

Describe. Describe the behaviour of concern in the most specific and objective terms possible. For example, 'When you allow Adam to stay up late at night . . .'.

Express or explain. Either express your feelings about the behaviour or explain the difficulties it causes for you, or do both, calmly and positively, without blaming or judging the other person, or 'putting them down'. For example, 'I get worried *(express)* because I can see he is tired the next day and finds it difficult to concentrate *(explain)*'.

Specify. Specify the exact change in behaviour required of the other person. For example, 'So, can you make sure he goes to bed by half past seven'.

Consequences. The consequences which are likely to result from the other person complying with the request are stated. The benefits for both people are stated along with any concessions which you are willing to make. For example, '. . . then Adam will not be tired at school and will make much better progress'. If the other person is not willing to comply, then the modified DESC script should be repeated, including the negative consequences for the person of not complying with the request.

Preparation and delivery. Although the modified DESC script is simple enough to be thought up and delivered on the spot it is often best to write it out beforehand. It is then possible to ensure the wording is suitable and also to rehearse it with a third person in order to get feedback on it. It can then be decided when, where and how it will be delivered.

Problem-solving and conflict resolution

Teachers often find that their opinions differ from those of parents or their colleagues. Where there is a serious conflict of opinions or needs it can lead to a deterioration in relationships unless these difficulties are resolved. A model for collaboration in solving problems or resolving conflicts (adapted from Bolton 1979) is outlined below.

- Define the problem from each person's perspective.
- Brainstorm possible solutions.
- Select solutions which meet both parties' needs.
- Plan who will do what, where and when.
- Implement the plan.
- Evaluate the process and the solution.

Further reading

Blamires, M., Robertson, C. and Blamires, J. (1997) *Parent–Teacher Partnership*. London: David Fulton Publishers.

Hornby, G. (1994) *Counselling in Child Disability: Skills for Working with Parents*. London: Chapman and Hall.

Hornby, G. (2000) *Improving Parental Involvement*. London: Cassell.

Wolfendale, S. (1992) *Empowering Parents and Teachers*. London: Cassell.

CHAPTER 13

Whole-school issues

Introduction

There are a number of issues concerning provision for pupils with SEN that relate to the way the school operates as a whole. These are issues that need to be addressed through the development of a whole-school SEN policy. This chapter provides guidelines for the development of such a policy and discusses some related issues including working with classroom assistants and other professionals, movement around school, special toileting facilities, relationships with other children, and the provision of opportunities for all children to participate in out of school activities.

Whole-school SEN Policy

Guidelines for the implementation of a whole-school policy on SEN must address a wide range of issues. These include:

- the principles and objectives which determine the policy and provision;
- the name of the school coordinator, responsible for its day-to-day management;
- arrangements to ensure the practices and responsibilities detailed are well coordinated;
- admission arrangements for pupils with SEN;
- details of any special facilities or expertise which can be offered in the school;
- arrangements made to allow physical accessibility to the school;
- the principles by which the resource allocation is made;
- the organisation of provision to identify, assess, monitor and review the progress of pupils with SEN;
- arrangements made to allow access to a broad, balanced and relevant curricular programme;
- approaches used to allow for pupils to participate as fully as possible in all school activities;
- the processes used for the evaluation of the school practices and procedures;

- arrangements in place for dealing with complaints;
- plans for staff development and in-service training;
- arrangements for asking for professional support from outside the school;
- arrangements made for developing partnerships with parents;
- details of links, either through staff or pupil participation, with other schools;
- details of links with outside agencies.

It is not the purpose of this book to deal with these features in detail and they have been summarised only briefly here. The *Code of Practice* (DfE 1994a) provides further details of the content for such a policy. Also, Hornby *et al.* (1995) discussed the strategies for its development, and provided examples of appropriate approaches to its implementation.

The school is required to have a policy document on SEN and this should be available in schools for parents and other interested parties to see. It is advisable that all staff should be acquainted with this document. The school SEN Coordinator should be able to provide you with a copy.

Working with classroom assistants

Some children with a Statement of SEN have time allocated for a classroom assistant to support them. Their Statement will allocate a number of hours for an assistant to work with them. The time allocated will be determined by the statementing panel and can vary from a few hours each week, working with a child in the classroom, to a full-time commitment, which also covers supervision at break and lunchtimes. The hours provided by the panel will reflect the level of the child's special educational needs.

The number of classroom assistants has risen sharply in the last few years and is expected to continue to rise in the next few years. The Government Green Paper *Excellence for All Children: Meeting Special Educational Needs* (DfEE 1997a) reported that there were over 24,000 classroom assistants working in mainstream schools in England, with another 16,000 employed in special schools. This was a number that the Government promised to increase significantly in the future.

Teaching staff with children with SEN in their classes are increasingly expected to work cooperatively with classroom assistants. Such arrangements can have a considerable bearing on the rate of development and the successful inclusion of pupils for whom it is provided. Furthermore, such cooperation can have an important bearing on the viability of arrangements that have been made in a child's Statement.

The role of the classroom assistant and their professional relationship with the class teacher are vital. The assistant needs to be well informed on a number of aspects of any lesson at which they are present. Many classroom assistants have little or no formal training to help them with their job and the classroom teacher is, of course, in overall control of the lesson and its direction and content. Consequently, teachers must be able to provide their assistants with a sense of direction and must work closely with them. The teacher's role is to design the appropriate learning programmes and that of the assistant to help to implement them.

An Audit Commission/HMI report (1992) maintained the key to effective support is good planning and communication. Fox (1993) identified three areas where support is important. These were support for the pupil, for the teacher and for the school. Panter (1995) identified three crucial questions concerned with the classroom assistant's role with the pupil in the classroom. These relate to an understanding of the objectives of the lesson in which they are present, the materials and resources to be used to support the lesson and the role that they will play in conjunction with the class teacher.

The relationship between teachers and assistants should be conducted on a 'two-way' basis. Despite their lack of formal training, classroom assistants can have helpful suggestions to make regarding children's work and progress, or have relevant knowledge of them in another situation that could be influential in future planning. Research conducted by Fox underlined the importance of a positive working relationship between teachers and classroom assistants. Teachers taking part in her survey indicated that the following factors were important:

- Classroom assistants are clear about their roles and responsibilities.
- They are aware of the learning implications of children's SEN.
- They are seen as being part of the school SEN team.

Beyond this, the survey conducted by Fox suggested that there must be time for planning, feedback and evaluation of their work together and that assistants must have time to develop their professional skills and knowledge.

It is also important that the work classroom assistants do is properly acknowledged in the school, as well as time being set aside to develop their skills and effectiveness. Balshaw (1999) is a particularly useful source of information for school-based in-service sessions with assistants.

Questions must also be raised as to the overall role of assistants in the classroom. It must be decided whether they should work with other pupils experiencing difficulties in the class or only with those designated. Ainscow (2000) suggests that best practice occurs when teachers are flexible, and the assistant, although focusing primarily on the needs of designated children for much of their time also spends time working with others who need help when this is appropriate.

Experience indicates that the rest of the pupils in the class resent one child monopolising the assistant and welcome the extra time which they can be given. Furthermore, if the assistant works with the whole of the pupil group this tends to benefit the social integration of the targeted pupil.

Government policy, identified in *Excellence for All Children* (DfEE 1997a) calls for a national framework for the training of all classroom assistants by 2002. There are an increasing number of nationally recognised qualifications for classroom assistants, some of which are competence-based National Vocational Qualification (NVQs) while others are assessed through more traditional approaches. Enquiries about the provision of such courses can be made through local further education colleges.

Additional help from other professionals

The most common forms of additional help needed by pupils with SEN are physiotherapy and speech therapy. In both cases the times for receiving this help will not be set by the teacher, and the child may have to leave lessons at times when it is inconvenient. Considerable cooperation and flexibility between various professionals is required so that classroom work can be completed with the minimum of disruption for all concerned.

The value of liaison with other professionals cannot be over-estimated. They will be able to provide a useful insight into the needs of individual children that may not manifest themselves in the classroom situation. In cases where they have worked with the child in a previous school they may be able to provide important background information. This will help to obtain a more comprehensive picture of the child. Exchanging information and views can also help to identify potential difficulties and promote the development of strategies to accommodate or even avoid difficulties.

Finding time to meet can be difficult, since therapists typically work in several schools during the week, but it is worth the effort.

Relationships with other children

The success of the school experience for some pupils with SEN can be gauged by their level of acceptance by others, both staff and pupils. This can be the first and most crucial hurdle. The attitudes of all staff in the school and staff arrangements will be vital. Important points regarding staff arrangements, and related questions, for the successful inclusion of pupils with SEN are:

- How is unsupervised time dealt with? Are pupils expected to get on as best they can or are other arrangements made for those with special needs? If other arrangements are made, are pupils who do not have special needs excluded? If they are excluded, what effect does this have on both parties?
- Mealtimes can be a traumatic experience for pupils with particular physical difficulties. If the canteen is self-service does that produce any problems? Some children have particular dietary restrictions. Are these dealt with in a thoughtful and considered way? How are those on free school meals treated; are they likely to be embarrassed by this?
- Special arrangements may be appropriate for some children when they are changing for games or PE. How does the school react to this situation? What solutions has it come up with?

Another key factor in the acceptance of pupils with special needs is the rationale used within the school to allocate them to classes. Key factors that need to be taken into consideration include:

- Do all the children with special needs, particularly learning difficulties, in the same year group end up in the same classes all the time? If they do, what effect does this have on them and their teachers?

- To what extent are other children in the class sympathetic and understanding? What is done to aid their understanding?
- Are the pupils with special needs withdrawn from the normal timetable arrangements at any time during the week and how is this justified?
- Is there a need for a programme specifically designed for some children to help them develop their skills? If there is such a programme, how is it organised and what personal benefits and costs might it have for participating pupils?

Movement around the school

Some children experience difficulties in getting around school and it is important that schools develop a policy to accommodate their needs. Some children's difficulties will relate purely to problems caused as a result of their disability, in other cases these problems will be worsened through the design of the building or perhaps its geographical layout.

In some circumstances it will be necessary that teachers allow particular children to be late for lessons. This may be necessary because of a difficulty in getting to the classroom. In other cases it may be necessary for a pupil to leave lessons early to be clear of the rush in the corridors. Sometimes specific arrangements may have to be made on behalf of pupils so that they are not late for examinations or tests.

The use of a trolley to help with the movement of a pupil's equipment can be useful. For some children who have difficulty in getting round school, a nurse or aide may be required. This may help in the overall movement of children during the day, and liaison between the teacher and the aide can be beneficial to all concerned to iron out any problems which may occur.

Special toileting arrangements

A small number of pupils have difficulties with their toilet arrangements. There are a number of conditions that demand that some children will need to go to the toilet at inappropriate times during a lesson. The difficulties this will cause to the pupil will vary according to the medical problem. This is an issue that all teachers should be made aware of, particularly the names of children for whom the normal toilet arrangements may be a problem.

From the class teacher's point of view, such disruptions to lessons are often irksome. Pupils can also find this a source of embarrassment. It is best, if at all possible, that a routine be worked out for visits to the toilet. The best times are of course break times and lunch times and if it is at all possible the routine should incorporate this pattern. It will be helpful to the pupil also if such a routine can be established. However, the routine must not be inflexible and there must be latitude in allowing a child who has problems to go to the toilet on request. In certain cases contact with parents, or even with the medical services, may be necessary.

The key factor to be kept at the forefront of the teachers' minds is the health and well-being of the child in question and their social acceptance among peers despite their difficulties.

Out of school activities

In order to encourage a feeling of full, personal integration, pupils with SEN need access to as many out of school activities as possible. On the other hand, in certain situations they may need to be counselled to dissuade them from participating in particular activities. However, on many occasions they will be able to participate in most things with a little planning by the staff concerned. Some of the factors which need to be taken into consideration include access to the mini bus, the need for extra or special medical supplies, extra clothing and/or food, the need (if relevant) for a wheelchair or folding chair, toilet stops and extra adult support to help. A useful guide on planning outdoor activities for the disabled is available (Croucher 1981).

Other whole-school issues

It is likely that schools will have developed 'whole-school' policies on a number of other issues. These might include bullying, discipline, assessment or curriculum planning. Teachers can therefore expect to work in cooperation with other colleagues in designing and implementing appropriate strategies for pupils with SEN.

An example of this is the responsibility for translating the principles of entitlement indicated in the Warnock Report into daily provision for all pupils. For pupils with SEN a key area to be addressed is for the development plan for individual subject areas to take into account their learning needs.

Similarly, all staff need to be informed of and involved in developing a whole-school assessment procedure. This will have common features relating to overall curriculum planning and both the formal and informal assessment procedures. Currently this will have to take into account the requirements of both external assessment and examination agencies.

Conclusions

Whole-school issues are precisely that and all school staff, not only the teachers, might expect to be involved in discussions which take place and the policy decisions that are made. The mechanisms for this vary greatly in individual schools, as do the topics to be considered. It is essential that you familiarise yourself with these in order to provide effectively for the children with SEN who you teach.

Further reading

Balshaw, M. H. (1999) *Help In the Classroom* (2nd edn). London: David Fulton Publishers.

Fox, G. (1998) *A Handbook for Classroom Assistants: Teachers and Assistants Working Together*. London: David Fulton Publishers.

Hornby, G., Davis, G. and Taylor, G. (1995) *The Special Educational Needs Coordinator's Handbook: A Guide for Implementing the Code of Practice*. London: Routledge.

Useful addresses

These are addresses of organisations and services concerned with children with special educational needs and who will provide information for teachers and other professionals.

ACT (Action for Children with Life Threatening Conditions)
65 St Michael's Hill,
Bristol BS2 8DZ
Tel: 0117 922 1556

ADD Information Services
Andrea Bilbow, PO Box, 340
Edgware Road, Middlesex HA8 9HL
Tel: 020 8905 2013
email: addiss@compuserve.com
website: www.addiss.co.uk

Advisory Centre for Education
1b Aberdeen Studios,
22–24 Highbury Grove,
London N5 2DQ
Tel: 020 7354 8318

Allergy Foundation, British
St Bartholomew's Hospital, West
Smithfield, London EC1A 7BE
Helpline: 020 7600 6166

Asperger's Syndrome: see Autism

Autistic Children, Scottish Society for
Hilton House, Alloa Business Park,
Whins Road Alloa FK10 3SA

Tel: 01259 720044
email: ssac@autism-in-scotland.org.uk

Autistic Society, The National
393 City Road, London EC1V 1NG
Tel: 020 7833 2299
email: nas@nasorg.uk

Autistic Society, The National (Scotland)
111 Union Street, Glasgow,
Strathclyde G1 3TA
Tel: 0141 221 8090
email: nas.scot.dev.fund@dial.pipex.com

Autistic Society, The National (Wales)
Suite C1, William Knox House,
Britannic Way, Llandarcy, Neath,
West Glamorgan SA10 6EL
Tel: 01792 815915
email: nas.wales.dev@dial.pipex.com

Centre for Studies on Integration in
Education (CSIE)
1 Redland Close, Elm lane,
Redland, Bristol BS6 6UE
Tel: 0117 923 8450

Deaf Children's Society, National (NDCS)
15 Dufferin Street, London EC1Y 8UR

Tel: 020 7250 0123
email: ndcs@ndcs.org.uk

Down's Syndrome Association
155 Mitcham Road, London SW17 9PG
Tel: 020 8682 4001
email: downs-syndrome.org.uk
website: www.downs-syndome.org.uk

Down's Syndrome Association, Scottish
158–160 Balgreen Road, Edinburgh
EH121 3AU
Tel: 0131 313 4225

Dyslexia Association, British
98 London Road, Reading,
Berks RG1 5AU
Tel: 0118 966 8271/2
email: info@dyslexiahelp-
bda.demon.co.uk
website: www.bda.demon.co.uk

Dyslexia Association, Scottish
Unit 3, Stirling Business Centre,
Wellgreen, Stirling FK8 2DZ
Tel: 01786 446650
email: dyslexia.scotland@dial.pipex.com

Dyslexia Institute
133 Gresham Road, Staines, Middlesex
TW18 2AJ
Tel : 01784 463851
email: dyslexia-inst@connect.bt.com
website: www.dyslexia-inst.org.uk

Dyspraxia Foundation
8 West Alley, Hitchin, Herts SG5 1EG
Tel: 01462 454986
website:
www.embrook.demon.co.uk/dyspraxia/

Emotional and Behavioural Difficulties,
Association for Workers for Children
(AWCEBD)

Mr Allen Rimmer, Charlton Court,
East Sutton, Maidstone,
Kent ME17 3DQ
Tel: 01622 843104
email: awcebd.mistral.co.uk
website: www.mistral.co.uk

Epilepsy Association, British
Anstey House, 40 Hanover Square,
Leeds, West Yorks. LS3 1BE
Tel: 0113 243 9393
email: epilepsy@bea.org.uk
website: www.epilepsy.org.uk

Fragile X Society, The
Mrs L Walker, 53 Winchelsea Lane,
Hastings, East Sussex TN35 4LG
Tel: 01424 813147
website: www.fragilex.org.uk

Gifted Children, National Association
for (NACE)
Elder House, Milton Keynes,
Bucks MK9 1LR
Tel: 01908 673677
email: nagc@rmplec.co.uk
website: www.rmplc.co.uk/orgs/nagc/

Health Education Authority
Trevelyan House, 30 Great Peter Street,
London SW1P 2HW
Tel: 020 7222 5300
website: www.hea.org.uk

Independent Panel for Special
Educational Advice (IPSEA)
John Wright, 4 Ancient House Mews,
Woodbridge, Suffolk IP12 1DH
Tel: 01394 380518

Learning Disabilities, British Institute of
(BILD)
Wolverhampton Road, Kidderminster,
Worcestershire DY10 3PP

Tel: 01562 851970
email: bild-irc.demon.co.uk
website: www.bild.org.uk

MENCAP
115–123 Golden Lane,
London EC1Y 0TJ
Tel: 020 7454 0454
email: mencap.plu@pipex.org.uk

MENCAP in Wales
31 Lambourne Crescent,
Cardiff Business Park Parc ty Glas,
Llanishen, Cardiff CF4 5GG
Tel: 029 2074 7588

MENCAP (Northern Ireland)
4 Annadale Avenue, Belfast BT27 5RB
Tel: 028 9069 1351

MIND (National Association for Mental
Health)
Granta House, 15–19 Broadway, London
E15 4BQ
Infoline (London) 020 8522 1728,
(nationwide) 0345 660163
website: www.mind.org.uk

Oasis
Brock House, Grigg Lane, Brockenhurst,
Hants SO42 7RE
Tel: 0891 633201
email: oasis@dial.pipex.com

Parent Partnership Network
John Khan, Council for Disabled
Children, 8 Wakley Street, London
EC1V 7QE
Tel: 020 7843 6058

Portage Association, National
127 Monks Dale, Yeovil,
Somerset BA21 3JE
Tel: 01935 471641

Royal National Institute for the Blind
(RNIB)
224 Great Portland Street,
London W1N 6AA
Tel: 020 7388 1266
email: webmaster@rnib.org.uk
website: www.rnib.org.uk/

RNIB Northern Ireland
40 Lindenhall Street,
Belfast BT2 8BG
Tel: 028 9032 9373
email: Mmcilwraith@rnib.org.uk

RNIB Scotland
Dunedin House,
25 Ravelston Terrace,
Edinburgh EH4 3TP
Tel: 0131 311 8500

Royal National Institution for Deaf
People (RNID)
19–23 Featherstone Street,
London EC1Y 8SL
Helpline: 0870 605 0123
website: www.rnid.org.uk

SENSE
11–13 Clifton Terrace, Finsbury Park,
London N4 3SR
Tel: 020 7272 7774

SKILL (National Bureau for
Handicapped Students)
366 Brixton Road,
London SW9 7AA
Tel: 020 7274 0565

Special Education Consortium
c/o Council For Disabled Children
8 Wakley Street,
London EC1V 7QE
Tel: 020 7278 9441

Special Educational Needs Information Service, The
Turner Library, Whitefield School and Centre, MacDonald Road, Walthamstow,
London E17 4AZ
Tel: 020 8531 8703 ext. 150
email: whitefield-edu@classic.msn.com

Special Educational Needs, National Association for (NASEN)
NASEN House, 4–5 Amber Business Park, Amington, Tamworth,
Staffordshire B77 4RP
Tel: 01827 311500
email: welcome@nasen.org.uk
website: www.nasen.org.uk

Stationery Office, The Publications Centre
51 Nine Elms Road,
London SW8 5DR
Tel: 020 7873 0011 (enquiries)
     020 7873 9090 (orders)
website: www.national-publishing.co.uk

There are a large number of other organisations and establishments working on behalf of children with special educational needs in the UK. A comprehensive list of addresses, email and website information is detailed in Worthington, A. (ed.) (1999) *The Fulton Special Education Digest: Selected Resources for Teachers, Parents and Carers*. David Fulton Publishers, Ormond House, 26–27 Boswell Street, London WC1N 3JZ.

References

Ablewhite, R. C. (1969) *Mathematics for the Less Able*. London: Heinemann.

Aherne, P. (1993) *Mathematics for All*. London: David Fulton Publishers.

Ainscow, M. (2000) 'Poor tactics let down Mums' army', *TES Research Focus* 31 March, p. 24.

Allan, J. and Nairne, J. (1984) *Class Discussions for Teachers and Counsellors in the Elementary School*. Toronto: University of Toronto Press.

Alston, J. and Taylor, J. (1987) *Handwriting: Theory, Research and Practice*. London: Croom Helm.

Audit Commission/HMI (1992) *Getting in on the Act: Provision for pupils with Special Educational Needs. The National Picture*. London: HMSO.

Ayers, H., Clarke, D. and Murray, A. (1995) *Perspectives on Behaviour. A Practical Guide to Effective Intervention by Teachers*. London: David Fulton Publishers.

Bailey, T. (1982) 'Mathematics in the secondary school', in M. Hinson and M. Hughes (eds) *Planning Effective Progress*. Amersham: Hulton/NARE.

Balshaw, M. H. (1999) *Help in the Classroom* (2nd edn). London: David Fulton Publishers.

Barthorpe, T. and Visser, J. (1991) *Differentiation: Your Responsibility – An in-service pack for Staff Development*. Stafford: NARE.

Bernstein, B. (1970) 'Pedagogies visible and invisible', in J. Karabil and A. H. Halsey (eds) *Power and Ideology in Education*. Oxford: Oxford University Press.

Best, A. B. (1992) *Teaching Children with Visual Impairments*. Milton Keynes: Open University Press.

Bloom, B. S. (1964) *Taxonomy of Educational Objectives: Handbook 1: Cognitive Domain*. London: Longman.

Bolton, R. (1979) *People Skills*. Englewood Cliffs, NJ: Prentice-Hall.

Booth, T. *et al.* (1992) *Learning for All (2): Policies for Diversity in Education*. London: Routledge.

Bower, S. A. and Bower, G. H. (1976) *Asserting Yourself*. Reading, Mass.: Addison-Wesley.

Brennan, W. K. (1985) *Curriculum for Special Needs*. Milton Keynes: Open University Press.

Bryant, N. D., Drabin, I. R. and Gettinger, M. (1981) 'Effect of varying unit size on spelling achievement in learning disabled children', *Journal of Learning Disabilities* 14, pp. 200–203.

Byers, R. (1999) 'The National Literacy Strategy and pupils with special educational needs', in *British Journal of Special Education* 26(1), pp. 8–11.

Chapman, E. K. and Stone, J. M. (1988) *The Visually Handicapped Child in your Classroom*. London: Cassell.

Charlton, T. and David, K. (eds) (1993) *Managing Misbehaviour in Schools*. London: Routledge.

Child, D. (1993) *Psychology and the Teacher*. London: Cassell.

Cockcroft, W. H. (1982) (Chair) *Mathematics Counts*. Report of the Committee of Enquiry into the Teaching of Mathematics in Schools. London: HMSO.

Cohen, L. and Manion, L. (1983) *A Guide to Teaching Practice*. London: Routledge.

Cole, T., Visser, J. and Upton, G. (1998) *Effective Schooling for Pupils with Emotional and Behavioural Difficulties*. London: David Fulton Publishers.

Coopersmith, S. (1968) *The Antecedents of Self-Esteem*. San Francisco: W. H. Freeman.

Cripps, C. C. (1983) 'A report on an experiment to see whether young children can be taught to write from memory', *Remedial Education* 18(1).

Croucher, N. (1981) *Outdoor Pursuits for Disabled People*. Cambridge: Woodhead Faulkner.

Dave, R. H. (1975) In R. J. Armstrong *et al. Developing and Writing Behavioural Objectives*. New York: Educational Innovation Press.

Dearing, R. (1993) *The National Curriculum and its Assessment: Final Report*. London: National Curriculum Council and School Examination and Assessment Council.

DES (Department of Education and Science) (1978) *The Warnock Report*. London: HMSO.

DES (1989) *A Curriculum for All*. London: HMSO.

DfE (Department for Education) (1994a) *Code of Practice on the Identification and Assessment of Special Educational Needs*. London: Central Office of Information.

DfE (1994b) *The Education of Children with Emotional and Social Difficulties (Circular 9/94)*. London: DfE.

DfEE (Department for Education and Employment) (1997a) *Excellence for All Children: Meeting Special Educational Needs*. London: DfEE.

DfEE (1997b) *Permanant Exclusions from Schools In England* (Press notice No. 30xi).

DfEE (1998a) *The National Literacy Strategy Framework for Teachers*. London: DfEE.

DfEE (1998b) *The National Literacy Strategy Framework for Teachers (Additional Guidance) on Children with Special Educational Needs*. London: DfEE.

DfEE (1998c) *Supporting the Target Setting Process. Guidance for effective target setting for pupils with special educational needs*. London: DfEE.

DfEE (1998d) *Special Needs: A Programme of Action*. London: DFEE

DfEE (1999) *The Daily Mathematics Lesson: Guidance for Professional Development*. London: DfEE.

Dolch, E. W. (1954) *A Manual for Remedial Reading*. London: Garrard.

Douglas, J. B. W., Ross, J. M. and Simpson, H. R. (1971) *All Our Futures*. London: Panther.

Egan, G. (1982) *The Skilled Helper* (2nd edn). Monterey, Calif.: Brooks/Cole.

Ellis, A. (1962) *Reason and Emotion in Psychotherapy*. New York: Lyle Stuart.

Fox, G. (1993) *A Handbook for Special Needs Assistants Working in Partnership with Teachers*. London: David Fulton Publishers.

France, N. (1979) *Profile of Mathematical Skills*. London: Nelson.

Galloway, D. *et al.* (1982) *Schools and Disruptive Pupils*. London: Longman.

Greenhalgh, P. (1994) *Emotional Growth and Learning*. London: Routledge.

Gribble, G. W. (1993) *Behaviour Management in Schools: a positive approach to discipline in Schools*. Bangor: School of Education, University of Wales.

Halliday, P. (1989) *Children with Physical Difficulties*. London: Cassell.

Haring, N. G. and Eaton, M. D. (1978) 'Systematic instructional procedures: an instructional hierarchy', in N. G. Haring *et al. The Fourth R: Research in the Classroom*. Ohio: Charles E Merill.

Haskell, M. and Barrett, E. (1993) *The Education of Children with Physical and Neurological Difficulties*. London: Chapman and Hall.

Haylock, D. (1991) *Teaching Mathematics to Low Attainers 8–12*. London: Paul Chapman.

Holland, S. and Ward, C. (1990) *Assertiveness: A Practical Approach*. Bicester: Winslow Press.

Hornby, G. (1994) *Counselling in Child Disability: Skills for Working with Parents*. London: Chapman and Hall.

Hornby, G. (1995) *Working with Parents of Children with Special Needs*. London: Cassell.

Hornby, G. (2000) *Improving Parental Involvement*. London: Cassell.

Hornby, G. Davis, G. and Taylor, G. (1995) *The Special Educational Needs Coordinator's Handbook. A Guide for Implementing the Code of Practice*. London: Routledge.

Hornsby, B. and Shear, F. (1990) *Alpha to Omega*. London: Heinemann.

Hughes, N. and Carpenter, B. (1991) 'Annual reviews: an active partnership', in R. Ashdown, B. Carpenter and K. Bovair (eds), pp. 209–222, *The Curriculum Challenge*. London: Falmer Press.

Jones, S. (1996) *In the Blood: God, Genes and Destiny*. London: Harper Collins.

Jordan, R. and Powell, S. (1995) *Understanding and Teaching Children with Autism*. Chichester: John Wiley and Sons.

Kelner, P. (1993) 'Happy families – are they a thing of the past?', *Sunday Times* 25 August.

Krathwohl, D. R. *et al.* (1964) *Taxonomy of Educational Objectives: Handbook 2: Affective Domain*. New York: McKay.

Kroth, R. L. (1985) *Communicating with Parents of Exceptional Children* (2nd edn). Denver: Love.

Kyriacou, C. (1991) *Essential Teaching Skills*. Oxford: Blackwell.

Lansdown, R. (1980) *More than Sympathy*. London: Tavistock.

Laslett, R. (1977) *The Education of Maladjusted Children*. London: Granada.

Leech, D. and Raybould, E. C. (1977) *Learning and Behaviour Difficulties in School*. London: Open Books.

McManus, M. (1989) *Troublesome Behaviour in the Classroom*. London: Routledge.

McNamara, S. and Moreton, G. (1995) *Changing Behaviour: Teaching Children with Emotional and Behavioural Difficulties in Primary and Secondary Classrooms.* London: David Fulton Publishers.

Macintosh, H. G. and Hale, D. E. (1976) *Assessment and the Secondary School Teacher.* London: Routledge and Keegan Paul.

Male, J. and Thompson, C. (1985) *The Educational Implications of Disability.* London: RADAR.

Manthei, M. (1982) *Positively Me: A Guide to Assertive Behaviour* (revised edn). Auckland, New Zealand: Methuen.

Martin, D. and Miller, C. (1996) *Speech and Language Difficulties in the Classroom.* London: David Fulton Publishers.

Mason, J. (1994) 'Assessing what sense pupils make of mathematics', in M. Sellinger (ed.) *Teaching Mathematics.* London: Routledge.

Meighan, R. (1991) *A Sociology of Education.* London: Cassell.

Miller, C. (1996) 'Sound Sense', *Special,* Spring, pp. 20–24.

Mitchell, C. and Koshy, V. (1993) *Effective Teacher Assessment.* London: Hodder and Stoughton.

Moore, M. and Wade, B. (1995) *Supporting Readers. School and Classroom Strategies.* London: David Fulton Publishers.

Mortimore, J. and Blackstone, T. (1983) *Disadvantage and Education.* Aldershot: Gower.

Mushinski-Fulk, B. and Stormont-Spurgin, M. (1995a) 'Spelling interventions for students with learning difficulties: a review', *Journal of Special Education* **28**(4), pp. 488–513.

Mushinski-Fulk, B. and Stormont-Spurgin, M. (1995b) 'Fourteen spelling strategies for students with learning difficulties', *Intervention in School and Clinic* **31**(1), pp. 16–20.

Nash, R. (1972) *Classrooms Observed.* London: Routledge and Keegan Paul.

National Curriculum Council (NCC) (1989) *National Curriculum Arrangements.* York: National Curriculum Council.

National Foundation for Educational Research (NFER) (1990) *Maths 7–11.* Windsor: NFER.

OFSTED (1993) *Handbook for the Inspection of Schools.* London: HMSO.

Panter, S. (1995) *How to Survive as a SEN Coordinator.* Litchfield: QEd.

Pedlow, H. (1999) 'The rise in mental disorders in adolescents'. Paper given to Homestart 25th Anniversary Conference. In R. Law and A. Rimmer (1999) *The Continuum of EBD.* Birmingham: University of Birmingham Distance Education Unit.

Peters, M. (1985) *Spelling: Caught or Taught* (2nd edn). London: Routledge and Keegan Paul.

Peters, M. and Cripps, C. C. (1983) *Appraisal of Current Spelling Materials.* Reading: Centre for the Teaching of Reading, University of Reading.

Portwood, M. (1999) *Understanding Developmental Dyslexia.* London: David Fulton Publishers.

Pressley, M. *et al.* (1990) *Cognitive Strategy Instruction that Really Improves Children's Academic Performance.* Cambridge, Mass.: Brookline Books.

Pumfrey, P. D. (1991) *Improving Children's Reading in the Junior School*. London: Cassell.

Reason, R. and Boote, R. (1994) *Helping Children with Reading and Spelling*. London: Routledge.

Reynolds, A. (1992) 'What is competent beginning teaching? A review of the literature', *Review of Educational Research* **62**(1), pp. 1–35.

Rogers, W. (1994) *Behaviour Recovery*. Melbourne: ACER.

Rosenthal, R. and Jacobson, L. (1968) *Pygmalion in the Classroom. Teacher Expectation and Pupils' Intellectual Development*. New York: Holt Renehart and Winston.

Rutter, M. and Smith, D. (1995) *Psycho-social Disorders in young People, Time, Trends and their Causes*. Chichester: John Wiley and Sons.

Rutter, M., Tizard, J. and Whitmore, K. (1970) *Education, Health and Behaviour*. London: Longman.

Rutter, M. *et al.* (1979) *15,000 Hours, Secondary Schools and their effects on Children*. Shepton Mallet: Open Books.

Sellinger, M. (1994) *Assessing in Mathematics, Teaching Mathematics in the Secondary School*, Mathematics Document 7. Milton Keynes: Open University Press.

Sewell, G. (1982) *Reshaping Remedial Education*. London: Croom Helm.

Sherliker, A. (1994) 'Integration into mainstream schools', *Special*, Spring pp. 38–43.

Slee, R. (1998) 'The politics of theorising special education', in C. Clark, A. Dyson and A. Millward *Theorising Special Education*. London: Routledge.

Smith, C. J. and Laslett, R. (1993) *Effective Classroom Management: A Teacher's Guide* (2nd edn). London: Routledge.

Solity, J. and Raybould, E. (1988) *A Teacher's Guide to Special Needs*. Milton Keynes: Open University Press.

Stakes, J. R. and Hornby, G. (1997) *Change in Special Education: What Brings it about?* London: Cassell.

Taylor, R. L. (1997) *Assessment of Exceptional Students* (4th edn). Boston: Allyn and Bacon.

Teacher Training Agency (TTA) (1999) *Career Entry Profile: Notes on Guidance and Standards*. London: Teacher Training Agency.

Tizard, B. and Hughes, M. (1984) *Young Children Learning*. London: Fontana.

Topping, K. S. (1983) *Education Systems for Disruptive Adolescents*. London: Croom Helm.

Tough, J. (1977) *Development of Meaning*. London: Allen and Unwin.

Ullman, L. and Krasner, L. (1965) *Case Studies in Behaviour Modification*. New York: Holt Reinhart and Winston.

Upton, G. (1983) *Educating Children with Behavioural Problems*. Cardiff: Faculty of Education, University College Cardiff.

Vincent, D. and Claydon, J. (1981) *Diagnostic Spelling Test*. Windsor: National Foundation for Educational Research.

Visser, J. (1999) *The Continuum of EBD (Distance Learning Module EDSE 06)*. Birmingham: University of Birmingham.

Visser, J. and Cole, T. (1996) 'An overview of English special provision for children with EBD', *Emotional and Behavioural Difficulties*, 1 March, pp. 11–16.

Visser, J. and Rayner, S. (1999) *Emotional And Behavioural Difficulties: A Reader*. Litchfield: QEd.

Waugh, D., Stakes, J. R. and Hornby, G. (2000) *Broad, Balanced and Relevant: Meeting the Needs of Children with Learning Difficulties Within the National Curriculum.* Hull: Halfacrown Academic.

Webster, A. and Elwood, J. (1985) *The Hearing Impaired Child in the Ordinary School.* Beckenham: Croom Helm.

Webster, A. and McConnell, C. (1987) *Children with Speech and Language Difficulties.* London: Cassell.

Webster, A. and Wood, D. (1989) *Children with Hearing Difficulties.* London: Cassell.

Westwood, P. (1993) *Commonsense Methods for Children with Special Needs* (2nd edn). London: Routledge.

Wheldall, K. (1991) 'Managing troublesome classroom behaviour in regular schools', *International Journal of Disability, Development and Education* **38**(2), pp. 99–116.

Wheldall, K. and Merrett, F. (1991) *Positive Teaching Packages.* Cheltenham: Positive Products.

Williams, H. (1999) Unpublished presentation to Distance Education EBD Course at University of Birmingham, 19 October.

Wilson, M and Evans, M. (1980) *Education of Disturbed Pupils.* London: Methuen.

Wolfendale, S. (1992) *Empowering Parents and Teachers.* London: Cassell.

Wolfendale, S. (ed.)(1993) *Assessing Special Educational Needs.* London: Cassell.

Index